BILL MORRISON

Bill Morrison has written extensively for the theatre, television and radio. His theatre work includes an adaptation of Hardy's *Tess of the D'Urbervilles* (Victoria Theatre, Stoke, 1971); *Patrick's Day* (Long Wharf, USA, 1972); *Sam Slade is Missing*, published in *Best Short Plays*, (ICA, 1973); *The Emperor of Ice Cream*, an adaptation of Brian Moore's novel, (Abbey Theatre, Dublin, 1977); *Flying Blind* (Liverpool Everyman, 1977 and Royal Court Theatre, 1978, nominated Evening Standard Best Play and Best Comedy Award, staged at the Harold Clurman Theatre, New York, 1979 and produced in Germany, Holland, Belgium, Norway, Sweden, Australia and New Zealand); *Scrap* (Liverpool Playhouse, 1981 and Half Moon Theatre, 1985); *Cavern of Dreams* with Carol Ann Duffy (Liverpool Playhouse, 1984); *Be Bop a Lula* (Liverpool Playhouse, 1988 and UK tour); *The Little Sister*, an adaptation of a Raymond Chandler novel (Liverpool Playhouse, 1991 and Plymouth Theatre Royal). He also directs and was joint Artistic Director of the Liverpool Playhouse from 1981-5. His television work includes: *McKinley and Sarah* and *Potato Head Blues* (both BBC 2); *Joggers* (BBC 1); *Shergar* (BBC Films); *A Safe House* (BBC 2 Screenplay); *Indelible Evidence* (BBC 2 Drama Documentary) and with Chris Ryder *Force of Duty* (BBC 2 Screenplay). His radio work includes: *The Love of Lady Margaret* (Radio 3); *The Spring of Memory* (Radio 4: Best Programme Pye Award, 1979), *Raymond Chandler Novels* (adaptation of six novels for Radio 4), an adaptation of *Crime and Punishment*, *The Great Gun-Running Episode; Maguire; Ellen Cassidy; Simpson and Son* and *Blues in a Flat*.

Other Volumes in this Series

A LOVE SONG FOR ULSTER

A Trilogy

BILL MORRISON

NICK HERN BOOKS
London

A Love Song for Ulster first published in Great Britain as an original paperback by Nick Hern Books, 14 Larden Road, London W3 7ST

The front cover picture, *Two Irishmen in W.11.*, by Lucian Freud, is reproduced by courtesy of the artist.

The review by Ann McFerran, *Forced Together*, which appeared in *The Times Literary Supplement* on 23rd April 1993 is reproduced by kind permission.

Typeset, printed and bound by Seagull Books, Calcutta, India

British Cataloguing in Publication Data

A catalogue record for this book is available from the British Library

ISBN 1-85459-260-2

1000643406

T

Contents

Forced Together

Two years ago, Tricycle artistic director Nick Kent invited Northern Irish writer Bill Morrison to write a play about contemporary Ireland. John Hume, the moderate Catholic SDLP leader inspired Morrison with an ingenious dramatic metaphor for this rich and complex trilogy.

Catholics and Protestants, the Irish politician said, were forced to live together in the same house. Ulster's problem is not just the 'arranged marriage' between the two but the seemingly interminable vexed questions and vested interests raised by the strings of in-laws on both sides which have produced the more intransigent and extreme factions.

A Love Song for Ulster chronicles the history of a family from the arranged marriage between John, a stolid, decent Protestant, and Kate, a beautiful, impetuous Catholic free spirit (superbly played by Brendan Coyle and Orla Brady) from the 1922 North-South partition to the recent bombings and atrocities which have brought about the round table power-sharing talks.

Morrison's trilogy about family conflict and bloody revenge is both a thrilling story and an exacting metaphor for the troubles. Just as Coppola's *Godfather* illuminates the psychology of the mafiosi power-politics of the United States, so Morrison's trilogy fluently demonstrates that Ulster's religious tribalism and rigid paternalism can mask a base fear and a primitive struggle for survival: the disenfranchised working-class Mick and Willy who appear like Beckettian furies have much more in common than the property-owning middle-class Catholics and Protestants.

Morrison's drama is packed with vibrant metaphor. Kate is raped by her brother-in-law, the dour Orange Victor, over the body of her dead husband, John; while the suffocation of the baby born of their idealistic civil rights offspring uncannily anticipates the callous outrage of Warrington, as it underlines the base hypocrisy of both Irish churches which appear at times to accept murder, but condemn abortion.

Although ultimately he ducks the role of the IRA, Morrison is at his best portraying the paradox of the Ulster Protestant who, as the fifties Ulster joke had it, was more loyal to the half crown than the Crown. Deploying a droll wit – and the trilogy is often very, very funny – and a steely dramatic analysis, Morrison reveals how the much derided working-class Protestants saw the 'troubles' as an opportunity to piggy-back on the Ulster evangelical church to become mafiosi-like racketeers interested only in prolonging the conflict, a horrendous and thuggish role which was quickly adopted by the IRA, and now dominates internal Northern Irish politics.

In the final play which deals with most recent history, the characters are too weighted down with their metaphorical baggage, but the first two plays are a triumph of consummate story-telling.

Invidious to single out performances in Nick Kent's triumphant production, but Val Lilley's feckless southern Irish Granny and Walter McMonagle's iron-faced preacher linger in the mind. Every young person tackling GCSE English, theatre studies or history should see this riveting piece. As someone who spent their first 20 years in Northern Ireland, I have never heard it explained so well, or with such compassion. Truly a love song for Ulster.

Ann McFerran
Times Educational Supplement, April 1993

A Selective Chronology from 1914

1914 Home Rule Act suspended for duration of World War 1.

1916 Easter Uprising in Dublin.

1920 Government of Ireland Act superseded Home Rule Act, but greater part of Ulster elected to remain united with Great Britain. Sinn Fein rejected the Act and a state of war existed between Ireland and England

1921 George V opened first Northern Ireland Parliament.

(Dec) Peace Treaty signed and Ireland partitioned. Irish Free State set up.

1922-1936 The Marriage

1922 Belfast: 257 Catholics killed. 11,000 lost their jobs. 23,000 forced out of their homes.
Royal Ulster Constabulary formed. Special Powers Bill enacted with rights to detain suspects and set-up courts of summary jurisdiction.
Michael Collins murdered by Republicans during Irish Civil War (1921-3).

1924 **(Feb)** Boundary commission (to adjust the Border) set-up on request of Irish Free State leader Cosgrave.

1925 General Election returns second Unionist Government under Craig as Prime Minister.
(Nov) Boundary commission report suppressed and functions of Council of Ireland transferred to Dublin and Belfast – Irish Free State released from obligation to contribute to reduction of UK National Debt.

1927 Republicans under de Valera renounce abstention from the Dail, and take their seats.

1929 Proportional Representation abolished in Ulster.

1932 De Valera (leader of Fianna Fáil) becomes President of Irish Free State.

1933 Special Powers Act made permanent in Ulster.

1936 Edward VIII abdicates. King George VI becomes King.

External Relations Act severs British Crown's relationship with Irish Free State except for formal diplomatic purposes.

1937 Irish Free State becomes Eire – a sovereign and democratic state with a new Constitution in which Articles 2 and 3 claimed national jurisdiction over whole island and Article 4 acknowledged 'special position' of Roman Catholic Church.

1938 British Government gives N. Ireland guarantee against budget deficits.
Chamberlain agrees to British Navy withdrawing from Eire's

five ports.

1939-1969 The Son

1939   IRA declared illegal by Eire government. Eire announces
policy of neutrality.
(Sept) Hitler invades Poland. UK declares war on Germany.

1940   Lord Craigavon (first Prime Minister of Northern Ireland)
dies in office.
(May) Winston Churchill becomes UK Prime Minister
(June) France signs Armistice with Germany
(July) De Valera rejects Churchill's cabinet offer of 'a
declaration of a United Ireland in principle, the practical
details to be worked out in due course; thus a united
Ireland to become at once a belligerent on the side of the
allies'.

1941   German air raids destroy 53% of Belfast's Housing stock.
100,000 flee Belfast.
(April/May) Fire engines sent from Dublin to Belfast to
help fight effects of Blitz.

1942   USA enters the war. US Naval Base Commissioned in Derry.

1943   120,000 Americans in N. Ireland prepare for Normandy
landings. 149 vessels based in Derry to patrol Western
approaches to UK.
Brooke becomes Prime Minister of N. Ireland.

1945   **(April)** De Valera signs condolence book at German
Embassy in Dublin after Hitler's suicide.
World War II ends.

1949   Eire becomes a republic – final break with the British
Monarchy.

1951   Harland & Wolff has a labour force of 21,000 of which less
than 4% are Catholics.
Ian Paisley co-founds Free Presbyterian Church.

1952   Free Presbyterians open first church building in Crossgar.

1956   Suez Crisis.
USSR invades Hungary.
'Rock around the Clock' becomes a world hit.

1957   De Valera re-introduces internment in Eire. 256 people
immediately interned.

1963   Pope John XXIII dies. Kennedy assassinated.
O'Neill becomes Prime Minister.
Ian Paisley fined for leading a demonstration against the

Lord Mayor of Belfast's decision to fly the Union Jack at half mast in sympathy for the Pope's death.

1964 Labour government elected under Harold Wilson.

1965 Sean Lemass (the Taioseach) meets O'Neill in Belfast. Civil Rights marches led by Martin Luther King in Montgomery, Alabama.

1966 Jack Lynch becomes Taioseach. Ian Paisley sets up Ulster Constitution Defence Committee with links to Ulster Protestant Volunteers.

1967 Ian Paisley demonstrates against Lynch's visit to the Stormont.

1968 Martin Luther King's march on Washington and 'I have a dream' speech.
First large civil rights march in N. Ireland. 2,500 people march from Coalisland to Dungannon.
(Oct) Derry Civil Rights march broken up by Police violence. World media attention focuses on Northern Ireland.
(Nov) O'Neill, Craig and Faulkner summoned by Harold Wilson to Downing Street where Wilson insists upon a five point plan of reforms (including a fair housing policy and universal suffrage in local elections). 'In 48 days of demonstrating the Catholic minority had won more concessions than they had in the last 48 years' *Jonathan Bardon: A History of Ulster*

1969 **(Jan)** Bogside barricaded and Radio Free Derry broadcasts.
(April) Ian Paisley imprisoned for illegal demonstration. Silent Valley reservoir blown up – IRA blamed (Later proved that the bombs were planted by Loyalists to discredit O'Neill's security policy and concessions towards the Catholic Community). O'Neill calls up 1,000 B specials and arms R.U.C.
O'Neill forced to resign because of hardening Unionist opinion. Chichester-Clark becomes Prime Minister of NI.
(Aug) Battle of the Bogside and riots in Belfast (10 killed, 745 injured).

1969-1993 The Daughter

1969 **(Aug)** Downing Street Declaration (agreed between Chichester-Clark and Harold Wilson) affirmed that 'Every citizen of Northern Ireland is entitled to the same equality of treatment and freedom from discrimination as obtains in the rest of the United Kingdom irrespective of political views or religion' and it reaffirmed 'That Northern Ireland should not cease to be part of the United Kingdom without the consent of the people of Northern Ireland . . . the border is not an issue.'

British troops put on the streets of Northern Ireland and the R.U.C. disarmed.

(Dec) Provisional IRA led by Sean McStiofian splits from the official IRA.

1970 (June) Bernadette Devlin elected to House of Commons. SDLP becomes principal voice for Catholic minority in Northern Ireland.

Conservative government elected under Edward Heath.

1971 (March) Chichester-Clark resigns having failed to obtain stronger security measures in London after protest march by Loyalist Shipyard Workers demands stronger action. Brian Faulkner succeeds him as Prime Minister.

(Aug) Internment introduced – 342 people immediately arrested.

(Sep) Ian Paisley calls for a third force to be set up, and simultaneously launches the Democratic Unionist Party which splits from the Ulster Unionist Party. Ulster Defence Association – a Loyalist Paramilitary organisation formed.

1972 (Jan) Bloody Sunday – 13 people killed by soldiers of the British Parachute Regiment during a demonstration march in Derry.

(Feb) 30,000 people march in Dublin to protest against the killings. The British Embassy burnt down. The official IRA carries the war to England. Five women, a Catholic padre and a gardener killed at Aldershot barracks.

(March) Edward Heath summons Faulkner to London to tell him Westminster will take over responsibility for Northern Ireland security. Faulkner immediately resigns; Heath prorogues Stormont for a year and Direct Rule is imposed. William Whitelaw is made Secretary of State for Northern Ireland.

(July) Bloody Friday. 39 bomb explosions over Northern Ireland kill 9 people and maim 130.

1973 (Jan) Internment of Loyalists for first time in over 50 years. The Irish Republic and the United Kingdom join the European Community.

(March) 57% vote YES in referendum to decide on whether Northern Ireland should remain in the United Kingdom. New constitutional arrangements for Northern Ireland published in White Paper from Westminister.

(Nov) Power-Sharing Executive elected by Proportional Representation takes office.

(Dec) Sunningdale Agreement sets up All-Ireland Council.

1974 **(Jan)** Ulster Unionist Council rejects All-Ireland Council, and Faulkner resigns as Unionist leader, but remains as leader of Power-Sharing Executive.
(Feb) British General Election after the Miners Strike, called by Edward Heath on question of 'who governs the country?' is turned into a referendum in Northern Ireland by the Vanguard and Official Unionist Parties, and 51% of the population vote against the Sunningdale agreement. Harold Wilson becomes Prime Minister.
(March) Merlyn Rees becomes Secretary of State for Northern Ireland.
(May) Ulster Workers's Council strike brings Northern Ireland to a halt, and after 2 weeks brings down the Power-Sharing Executive.
(July) Direct Rule re-introduced.

1976 **(Aug)** 20,000 people attend Peace Rally in Ormeau Park organised by Peace People founded by Mairead Corrigan and Betty Williams.
(Sept) Pope John Paul II's visit to Ireland. At Drogheda he says: 'On my knees I beg you to turn away from the paths of violence and return to the ways of peace'.

1979 Margaret Thatcher becomes Prime Minister of the U.K. Humphrey Atkins becomes Secretary of State for Northern Ireland.
Airey Neave assassinated by IRA bomb in House of Commons car park.
Lord Mountbatten and members of his family killed by IRA bomb outside Mullaghmore Harbour.

1981 **(March)** H Block hunger strike begins led by Bobby Sands, campaigning for restoration of political status for IRA prisoners.
(April) Sands, while in prison, is elected to Westminster in by-election for Fermanagh and South Tyrone.
(May) Sands, dies, and in the next 3 months nine other hunger strikers die.
(Oct) Hunger strike campaign is called off by the Provisional IRA.

1984 **(Oct)** Brighton bombing kills 5 people at the Conservative Party Conference.

1985 **(Nov)** Anglo-Irish Agreement signed by Margaret Thatcher and Garrett Fitzgerald at Hillsborough.
20,000 demonstrate against Anglo-Irish Agreement in Belfast led by Ian Paisley and Jim Molyneux. The Democratic Unionist Party and the Official Unionist Party withdraw from all local councils and start campaign of 'non co-operation'.

1986   **(April)** Molyneux and Paisley unveil 12 point plan of civil disobedience against the Anglo-Irish agreement.

1987   **(Jan)** Unionists present a petition with 400,000 signatures against the Anglo-Irish Agreement to the government at Westminster.
Belfast Council fined £25,000 for failing to set a rate as part of the Unionist Campaign of non co-operation – as a result the campaign begins to crumble.
(Nov) Bomb at the Rememberance Day Service at Enniskillen kills 11 people and injures 63.
The Dail introduces fresh legislation to expedite the extradition of terrorists.

1989   **(Nov/Dec)** Berlin Wall dismantled. Brandenburg Gate opened.

1990   **(Jan)** Secretary of State Brooke undertakes a series of bilateral discussions ('talks about talks') with four main constitutional parties in N. Ireland.
(Oct) German re-unification.

1991   **(June)** Opening of substantive talks – Democratic Unionist Party walks out after one hour, complaining that the SDLP and Alliance had been willing to begin Strand One of talks before the DUP had accepted the chair for Strand Two. They return after agreeing Chairman for Strand Two talks.
(July) Talks end with no date set for their resumption.
(Oct) Northern Ireland's first purpose built post-primary school to educate young people irrespective of religious belief formally opened.

1992   **(Jan)** Dissolution of the Soviet Union. State of Croatia achieves independence.
(March) Peter Brooke and party leaders meet at Stormont to begin new talks.
(April) British General Election returns John Major as Prime Minister. Bosnia Hercegovina recognised as independent state by European Community and by United States in July.
(July) Opening plenary session of Strand Two talks takes place in London then moves to Belfast. Opening plenary meeting of Strand Three talks takes place in Dublin.
(Nov) Statement issued on behalf of talks participants announcing that although the talks did not result in a comprehensive accommodation of the N. Ireland problem the participants had discussed most, if not all, of the elements which would comprise a general settlement and developed a clear understanding of each others positions. Sir Patrick Mayhew makes statement reiterating the

sentiments of the joint statement and the Government's
determination to persevere with dialogue.

Notes on Staging

The plays can be performed by a company of 11 actors (8 men and, I regret, only 3 women) and a band.

The place is a house set in a landscape, the ownership of which is constantly in dispute. Therefore its boundaries are of great importance. The symbolic defined space matters much more than the furnishings which should be basic. The table is the centre of the action.

The story begins in the 1920's and moves forward in time to today. Costume should reflect this but some elements are almost unchanging and resist fashion. They are all, and should be seen as, uniforms having an emblematic life.

What matters most is that the place defined is a constant prison for the flow of the action.

MICK and WILLIE begin the plays as ghosts, become real, and end as ghosts again.

The band should be in a place where they can be seen and contribute to the action. I have only indicated some specific places for music but it should be developed to underscore the action and reflect the strong rhythmic changes in popular music over the period, the outside world of dance bands, records and the radio rather than traditional Irish music.

A LOVE SONG FOR ULSTER

A TRILOGY

A Love Song for Ulster was first staged at the Tricycle Theatre, London on 27 March, 1993 with the following cast:

WILLIE	Alan McKee
MICK	John Elmes
THE SERGEANT	Dennis Conlon
THE OFFICER	Terry Mortimer
MARY	Val Lilley
KATE	Orla Brady
GABRIEL/SOLDIER	Darragh Kelly
JOHN/BOYD	Brendan Coyle
VICTOR	John Keegan
PRIEST/HIS REV	Walter McMonagle
ANNE	Anna Livia Ryan
MUSICIANS	Donovan Carpenter and Heather Joyce

Director Nicolas Kent
Designer Bunny Christie
Musical Director Terry Mortimer
Lighting Designer David Colmer

PLAY ONE: THE MARRIAGE

ACT ONE

WILLIE *and* MICK *begin the play.*

As they talk they carry out, through and round the house bags, bundles, household items, the baggage of an evacuation. They pile them to one side.

WILLIE. Mick?

MICK. What?

WILLIE. I've been thinking.

> MICK *drops his bundle, closes his eyes. Takes a deep breath.*

MICK. Why do you want to do that?

WILLIE. I can't help it.

MICK. Try. Just try not to.

WILLIE. I can't stop myself.

MICK. You'd think . . . you'd think we'd at least get a rest from thinking. But no. On it goes. Give it up. And shut up.

> *Silence as they get on with it.*

WILLIE. Do you not want to know what I'm thinking?

MICK. Willie . . . I told you . . .

WILLIE. All right, let me just ask you a question. Just to pass the time. All right?

MICK. What?

WILLIE. Right. Do you know your bible?

MICK. What?

WILLIE. That's what I've been thinking about.

MICK. You? The bible?

WILLIE. I can read. You see what I've been thinking about . . .

MICK. What's your question?

WILLIE. It's this. Why Abraham and Isaac?

MICK. What kind of a frigging question is that?

WILLIE. No, what I mean is, why the story? That's what bothers me. Why's it there?

MICK. Because it happened.

WILLIE. Ah but did it?

MICK. The bible says it did.

WILLIE. But you and I know that what's said and what happened can be two very different things.

MICK. What's your problem?

WILLIE. It doesn't make sense.

MICK. That's probably because you can't read the long words, like father, unfamiliar words like that.

WILLIE. I knew my father. I just never saw him. No, it's the boy that bothers me. Isaac, son of Abraham.

MICK. So what about him?

WILLIE. He's a right frigging puzzle is Isaac. I mean, why did he do it, why did he go along with it? Or did he not do it and they're only saying he did do it.

MICK. I thought Abraham did it.

WILLIE. Oh he started it. Well, actually God started it. God dropped the word in Abraham's ear and said – Away you go and take your son Isaac up that mountain. That's how it started. Isaac's working away at whatever he's doing and the Da calls him over. C'mere son, he says, you're coming with me. Now it doesn't record what Isaac said to this but it was probably along the lines of – Why, where are we going, Da?

MICK (*sighs*). I might have known.

WILLIE. What?

MICK. That you'd be bound to get the wrong end of the stick. If it doesn't record it then it didn't happen.

WILLIE. That's bollocks.

MICK. It's history.

WILLIE. I know about history. History always leaves out what people felt about it while it was happening. It always leaves out that most people didn't like it, didn't want it, protested about it and were generally fucked by it.

MICK. That's because it never made any difference to the final result. But this is different anyway.

WILLIE. For why?

MICK. Because this is the bible. It's the truth. It's holy writ.

WILLIE. And you believe that?

MICK. I don't have to. The thing's obvious. He was a good and obedient son like they were in them days and if the Da said go he went. The reason it's not recorded is because he said nothing.

WILLIE. Not even to say where are we going? C'mon.

MICK. He would have got a clip round the ear. He wouldn't have dared open his gob. The oul Da was a hard man.

WILLIE. All right, he might have said nothing then but wait till you see what happens next. Abraham takes Isaac, his only son mind you, he takes him, a couple of tribesmen and two asses, and they all set off. And they gather up wood as they go. Three days later they get to the land of Moriah and Abraham turns round to the fellas and says, this is as far as you go, you stay here with the asses, me and the lad are going on to worship. Then he loads Isaac up with the wood, takes the fire in one hand and a knife in the other and they set off up the mountain. Now. Now Isaac speaks. He's started putting two and two together so he says – and it records this in the story – he says to the Da . . . Da, we've got the fire and we've got the wood but where's the lamb for the burnt offering?

MICK. It's a reasonable question. What did the Da say?

WILLIE. He says – My son, God will provide himself with a lamb for a burnt offering. And they go on. Now, from here on in it does not record that Isaac said another dicky bird.

MICK. So?

WILLIE. Are you going to tell me that has to be true because it's holy writ?

MICK. Why not?

WILLIE. C'mon. Isaac has started putting two and two together. Now the Da's not giving him a straight answer. He's got that funny look in his eye he gets when he's hearing the voices. They're all alone out in the wilderness and the Da is piling the wood up into a sacrificial altar. Isaac questions it before, but when the Da grabs him and ties him down on the altar and he realises he's the frigging sacrifice apparently he doesn't open his mouth.

MICK. What's odd about that?

WILLIE. He doesn't even resist.

MICK. There was no point in saying anything. It's too late. This is his Da. He has the grindstone out and the sparks are flying off the knife. He's added up the two and two and whichever way he tries it the answer comes out, you're fucked. What's he going to say? Excuse me dearest pater, please think on what you do?

WILLIE. I'd say it was worth a try.

MICK. Maybe. If the Da was thinking. But the Da's not thinking. His mind is on higher things. He's hearing the funny voices which must be obeyed. Do what the Lord commands, destiny calls. I am the chosen one, all that. So the story's not wrong. He didn't say anything. What could he do?

WILLIE. Well . . . he could go over the Da's head. He could appeal to the boss.

MICK. What, pray? Pray to God? It was God that put the contract out on him. No chance.

WILLIE. He could fight back.

MICK. The Da's bigger and stronger.

WILLIE. He could have made a run for it.

MICK. Where? There's thickets all around. Where's he going to run? He's three days away from home. No, the only chance he ever had was blown by then.

WILLIE. What chance?

MICK. That when God first put it to Abraham, sacrifice your only son to show you love me, that Abraham would have turned round and said – Fuck off, God, you're not having him, what kind of a shit deal is that?

WILLIE. Nobody said – Fuck off, God – in the old Testament.

MICK. Exactly. And we've been paying for it ever since. There was nothing Isaac could say or do so he did and said nothing.

WILLIE. I don't believe it. I just don't believe that's the whole story.

MICK. Abraham didn't give a damn about Isaac. When it came down to it between God and son it was no contest. There's only one God but what's a son here or there. Abraham only had to get a couple more wives and get stuck into some serious begatting.

WILLIE. The boy must have done or said something. I mean, he's sussed the form, the fire, the knife, the altar, no sacrificial flesh in sight except his own. He would at least have said – Da, are you hearing those funny voices again? Wouldn't you like to lie down in the shade for a bit? Just give me the knife and I'll cut myself free and bring you a drink of water. Then I'll have a wee look round, there's probably a lamb round here somewhere, we just haven't seen it. Stuff like that.

MICK. He didn't.

WILLIE. Do you know what I think? He did, but the old men who were telling the story left it out because it didn't suit them.

MICK. He didn't get sacrificed either. God relented at the last minute.

WILLIE. Ah but that was just the happy ending to make it a better commercial.

MICK. Aye, to show God was good.

WILLIE. Oh no.

MICK. What then?

WILLIE. To show the rewards of blind obedience. That's why the story is not interested in what Isaac felt. He's just there to show that even with his own father's knife at his throat he submitted to the authority of his earthly father backed up by his heavenly father. A good loyal son. It works too. It fooled me for a long time.

MICK. Well what do you think Isaac should have done?

WILLIE. He should have kicked Abraham in the goolies the minute he started coming at him with the knife and the rope.

MICK. It was his father.

WILLIE. Who needs a fucking father like that?

MICK. It was his father with God on his side.

WILLIE. It was two men on a mountain top and the one with the knife is hearing voices saying – Kill, kill. That is no time for frigging theology. That is when you kick him in the nuts and run.

MICK. But by doing that you reject God and his earthly authority.

WILLIE. Which is why the story must be a cover up of the real events. What kind of an Old Testament would you have if in the very first book a son kicked his Da in the bollocks and took the knife off him? That's why it has to show Isaac as a jellybaby. It doesn't mention how his mother felt about her only son being taken off like that or what she might have done about it. Ever think of that?

MICK. Ever think about how many mothers have sent sons off to wars since?

WILLIE. Fair enough. I'll give you that.

MICK. So you think the son should rebel and start telling the old men what to do?

WILLIE. It's better than being carved up like the Christmas turkey.

MICK. You have it all wrong.

WILLIE. Oh you would say that.

MICK. You have.

WILLIE. How?

MICK. You have based your whole argument on the supposition that Isaac has only got one choice – between lying there meek and mild and getting his throat cut, or getting up and fighting his father. Right?

WILLIE. Right.

MICK. And did the story turn out like that?

WILLIE. Well . . . no . . .

MICK. No, it didn't because that's not what it's about. Isaac was never in danger. It was God testing Abraham. All Isaac had to do was trust his Da. Kicking him in the plums would have just cocked it up.

WILLIE. It would have done that all right.·

MICK. So Isaac did the right thing. He shared his father's belief. He did what his father wanted him to do. He kept the faith. He knew it would turn out all right in the end.

WILLIE. Oh yeah? Well, we'll see, won't we?

A SERGEANT *comes on and puts down a large box, centre, then stands guard beside it.* WILLIE *and* MICK *move to the side.*

Mind you, it has taught me one thing.

MICK. What's that?

WILLIE. Be bloody careful of anyone who claims they're acting on the instructions of a higher power. They may seem normal but you are in the presence of someone who is hearing funny voices and has a knife behind their back. And they are most probably your father or your mother.

MICK. I won't hear a word against my mother. She never hit us unless we deserved it. She was a saint with what she had to put up with.

WILLIE. What was that?

MICK. It was the way my Da kept laying me out on the kitchen table and asking her to bring the carving knife. And that was just to get me to go to school.

WILLIE. Nice one. Here they are.

A line of people come on. Among the crowd are MARY, her son GABRIEL and her daughter, KATE. A ragged assembly. The OFFICER appears and gets up on the box.

OFFICER. Right. Pay attention. I will keep this short and simple. It has to be simple for you bloody lot to understand it. You are all a pain in the arse. We are fed up with you. So. We are going to divide this island. Those of you who are loyal to the Empire and want to stay within it can have the North and the rest of you who demand independence can have your own country in the South. Provided. Provided you remain allied to the Empire in case we ever need you. Right. That's it. Carry on, Sergeant.

Gets down and goes off.

SERGEANT. Right, you lot, shift yourselves.

He herds them towards the baggage which they pick up.

You, you lot, on your way out there. You lot get back in there.

Some go back through the house. The rest trail off at the side heading south. The last are MARY, GABRIEL and KATE. A bag left by the house.

MARY. Kate, would you get that bag of yours over there.

KATE goes back to get it. As she turns to come back to her mother the SERGEANT steps out and blocks her path.

SERGEANT. And where are you going?

KATE. That's my mother over there. I want to go with her.

SERGEANT. Sorry, the line's been drawn. You can't cross it.

KATE. But I don't want to be here. I want to be with the rest.

SERGEANT. You're left in the North. That's the way the line's been drawn.

KATE. Then redraw the bloody line.

SERGEANT. Sorry, love, I didn't make the rules.

KATE. Let me through.

SERGEANT. You'll be better off here. What are you doing tonight?

KATE. Listen, you long string of shite, don't you give me orders in my own home. Isn't that what we fought you for? Let me through.

SERGEANT. Piss off, darling.

KATE. Mother, mother, he won't let me past. Come and tell him. Ma, come and get me, come and tell him.

MARY (*waving*). Goodbye, darling.

KATE. What?

ARY. I said, goodbye darling. I have to get on now. It's all for the best. C'mon, Gabriel.

She loads the bags on him and they prepare to go.

KATE. Ma. Come back here. Ma.

SERGEANT. You see, she doesn't want you. I'm not surprised with the mouth you have on you.

KATE. Ah go and stuff your tits in a mangle. Ma. Come here. Let me talk to her. Ma, you can't leave me here.

SERGEANT. Here, missus, you explain it. I'm not getting involved in it.

He stands aside. MARY *approaches reluctantly.*

MARY. It's all been aranged. There's nothing I can do about it.

KATE. What's been arranged?

MARY. You heard what the officer said.

KATE. But I don't want to stay in the North.

MARY. Some of us have to.

KATE. Why? Why me?

MARY. We have to be going now. (*Turning away.*)

KATE. But . . .

GABRIEL. Ma, we shouldn't leave her.

MARY. Will you hold your tongue, Gabriel. Don't you question your elders and betters. They know best. We all have to make sacrifices.

KATE. Mother, why are you betraying me?

MARY (*coming back*). Will you keep your voice down and don't make a show of me.

KATE. I could kill you.

MARY. Will you keep her off me?

SERGEANT *steps forward.*

It's typical of you. Always ungrateful. From the day you were born you had my heart scalded.

KATE. Let me at her.

SERGEANT. You're staying here.

MARY. You heard what the man said.

KATE. I don't want any part of his Empire. I'm not safe here.

MARY. You have nothing to fear. That's been guaranteed. It has all been arranged. (SERGEANT *steps back.*)

KATE. What has been arranged?

MARY (*talking low*). Isn't this still our true home. Hasn't somebody to be here to claim it when the time is right? This is your inheritance. This land can be yours one day. You have to stay. (*Louder.*) Now remember to say your prayers and whatever you do don't forget your faith.

KATE. It's not prayers I need.

As she looks and sees JOHN come on wearing long johns and polished black boots. Accompanied by MICK and WILLIE who carry all that is needed to dress him ritually in the regalia of an orangeman. White shirt, stiff collar, black tie, black suit, braces and belt, white gloves, medals, an orange sash, and last of all a black bowler hat the necessary one size too big.

MARY. Think of it as a blessed event. A marriage. What every woman wants. A husband and a home. It's time you were making your own home.

KATE. I want my own choice.

MARY. The men have decided.

KATE. Then to hell with the men.

MARY. You'll soon learn that what the men want the men will have and we can do nothing but submit to it. With modesty and prayer. We all have to make sacrifices.

KATE. I want to make my own choice.

MARY. You can't fly in the face of God.

KATE. What has God to do with it?

MARY. Hush your wicked tongue.

KATE (*looking at* JOHN). Have you any money on you?

MARY. What for?

KATE. So that I can buy a ticket out of here.

MARY. You know we have no money at all.

KATE. Mother, what have you done to me?

MARY. The best I can for you. I can hardly feed all I have never
mind a grown girl with the appetite of a young horse and a
mouth that would blister paint. It has been arranged and
there's an end of it. And maybe now we can have some peace.
That's all I want. Some peace. I'll pray for you. C'mon, Gabriel,
we have to go.

GABRIEL. Can I say goodbye to my sister?

MARY. Aye, but hurry.

She moves off to wait as GABRIEL *approaches* KATE. SERGEANT
steps forward.

GABRIEL. I'm only saying goodbye to her.

SERGEANT *steps back.*

KATE. Gabriel, I'm afraid for my life here.

GABRIEL. Don't worry. This division won't last. There are some of
us haven't given up and won't give up till the whole island is
ours.

KATE. Will you come for me? Do you promise? I have no one to
protect me here.

GABRIEL. Aren't I your brother? I'll be back. That's a promise.

She kisses him.

SERGEANT. That's enough then. Away you go.

MARY *hurries to grab* GABRIEL. *Thrusts a small prayer book and a
small Irish flag on a stick at* KATE.

MARY. Here. Your dowry for you. Now I have a family to attend to.
It's best not to think, daughter, for thought only breaks the
helpless heart. Pray. Goodbye. God bless you.

She and GABRIEL *go off.*

By now JOHN *is dressed and* MICK *and* WILLIE *stand back.* JOHN
walks off and they follow.

SERGEANT. Would you come out with me tonight?

KATE. I wouldn't piss on you if you were on fire. Now get out of here. If this is going to be my home then it will be mine and not yours.

He goes off. Alone. Then all the tense sadness shows. But pulls herself together. Finds a bucket and scrubbing brush and attacks the plain wood table, scrubbing as if her life depended on it. As she finishes and it darkens JOHN, *still, in his regalia but well tousled now, reels in.*

JOHN. Hello, wife. How's about you?

She gives him a stony look. He takes a bottle from his pocket, gets two glasses, sets them all on the table.

Will you have a drink with me?

She puts the bucket and brush down.

That's good. I like a clean house. Here. Will you take these off me?

Holds out his hands with the white gloves. She considers, decides not to make an issue of it. Walks over and slowly peels off the gloves and puts them on the table. He sits and stretches out a boot. She walks away from him. He looks after her and sees where she has put down prayer book and flag. Goes and lifts flag.

What's this?

KATE. It's mine.

He breaks it in two and throws it down.

JOHN. There'll be none of that in this house. It's you and me for it. Like it or no.

Sits again. Pissed but in amiable mood. Doesn't want to get off on the wrong foot. He's not a bad man.

Sit down and have a drink with me. Come on. You and I will get on right well together. If we understand each other. Come on. Have a drink.

Pours out two, watching her. She doesn't move towards him. He eases his boots off, takes a gulp of his drink.

Come and sit down here. Take your drink. You and me'll be fine together. Whatever you want, it'll be yours. It's a good home. There's all we need. Sit down. Will you not speak to me? Kate?

KATE. I don't know you.

JOHN. I'm simple enough. I'm the son of the son of the son of the son of some poor gam who was washed over from Scotland and stayed. Worked till they dropped. Built where there was nothing. Trusted nobody. Danced to nobody's tune. Believed that each man was his own conscience. Thought perversity was a virtue. A man of the North. Proud of it. And that's what you are now, a woman of the North.

KATE. Am I?

JOHN. They left you here. They didn't go on fighting for you. You were the sacrifice. Agh, come on, sit down, take a drink, we'll sing a song, forget it all. Be just you and me. In our own place.

KATE. I already have a home.

JOHN. Your home is here now, with me.

KATE. I had no choice of that.

JOHN. Well, neither did I.

KATE. Would you for God's sake take off that bowler hat?

JOHN. I'm sorry . . . I'm sorry . . . where's my manners? . . . I'm sorry . . .

Grabs it off and pitches it away.

KATE. And that stupid scarf.

JOHN. Scarf? This is no scarf. This is the sash my father wore.

He takes it off, looks at it.

I'll tell you something. I'll tell you something I never told anybody. I thanked God the day he died. I was like a bird set free. Oh I mourned him but inside, inside I was like spring water. He was a bitter hard man. Always had the knife in you. Beat me to make me obedient, the bible in one hand, his stick in the other. Because it was good for me. He was as soft as the flints on the market road. To him I could never live up to him and his inheritance. I had to be made to be worthy of it. I'm sure he wished my younger brother, Victor, had been born the elder. But he was stuck with me. And I'm not him. Fold that up for me and put it away, don't let it lie between us.

KATE. I don't want to touch it.

JOHN. All right.

He puts it in his pocket. Takes a drink, puts his jacket on the back of the chair. Collar and tie off. Pushes the other glass towards her.

Here.

She comes slowly over, lifts glass, sips.

Sit, lass sit.

She does. He relaxes.

We're rightly now. Here, have a wee drop more. (*Pours.*) Now, tell me this.

KATE. What?

JOHN. Can you cook?

KATE (*laughs*). I can.

JOHN. Thank God for that. Since my Ma died I've been eating Victor's stew. Can you bake? Soda Bread?

KATE. Yes.

JOHN. Potato bread?

KATE. Yes.

JOHN. Pancakes, wheaten farls, and wee sweet scones.

KATE. Yes.

JOHN. Champ with scallions and butter.

KATE. Fit for a king.

JOHN. I can taste it now.

KATE. Pork, ribs, broth, bacon and cabbage. A boiled brown egg for your breakfast. Porridge in the winter. Fish on Friday.

JOHN. Not in this house.

KATE. It is what my religion decrees.

JOHN. All right. Civil and religious liberty here, that's what we stand for. Could we have herrings, fried in oatmeal with new spuds?

KATE. Trout in butter, salmon baked in a pastry . . .

JOHN. Oh stop. We can make a go of it, you and me. Come over here and sit by me.

KATE. When I'm ready.

JOHN. Come on here now.

KATE. When I want to.

JOHN. Have another drink. It'll put you in the mood.

KATE. No.

JOHN. Go on. (*Pouring.*) Where's the harm in it.

KATE. I'm tired. It has been enough for one day.

JOHN. The night's young. Drink. To please me.

Reluctantly she sips.

We'll get on.

A silence. He drinking, looking at her. The next question hangs between them. He yawns, he stretches, exaggerating it. She gets up.

KATE. I'd like to go to bed now.

JOHN (*getting up*). Grand. We'll go now then.

KATE. I want to go alone.

He sits down again.

JOHN. Why would you want to do that?

KATE. I'm tired.

JOHN. But it's you and me, Kate, together.

KATE. It was not my choice.

JOHN. It's done now. It's been arranged, signed and sealed.

KATE. Not by me.

JOHN. We get on. You can see we'll get on.

KATE. I want to go to sleep.

JOHN. Can we not get on? Surely we can.

KATE. Maybe.

JOHN. Well then, let's you and me go to bed. Sign it and seal it.

KATE. Not tonight.

JOHN. Then when?

KATE. I don't know.

JOHN. You don't have to be afraid of me.

KATE. I am.

JOHN. I don't want you to be. This is your home now. With me.

KATE. And if I don't want it to be?

JOHN. It's not what we want, it's what we've got.

KATE. I want a choice.

JOHN. We make the best of it together.

KATE. It is my choice.

JOHN. Not in my house.

KATE. Can I go to bed now?

JOHN. You're not being wise.

KATE. I have a home. And they will come for me, to take me back, in time, when they are able. They will come for me.

JOHN. They won't.

KATE. They will.

JOHN. They left you here.

KATE. They did not.

JOHN. They weren't forced to do it. They gave you up.

KATE. They were forced. My brother will come for me.

JOHN. They gave you up, Kate, and left you to me.

KATE. I didn't choose you.

JOHN. No more did I choose you. None of us got our choice in the end.

KATE. You got what you wanted.

JOHN. Oh aye, I got what I wanted. I was allowed to keep my own land and not have it taken from me. My neighbour has become my enemy. And I have you standing in my kitchen. I'm spoiled for choice. But that's the way it is now.

KATE. No.

JOHN. We only have one choice. To make the best of it.

KATE. No.

JOHN. I am not a bad man. Cast an eye around you. There's sweet grass in the field, the beasts are fat, the hens are laying, butter churning. Crops growing. Markets to give us a good price. Factories and workers to feed. Plenty. If we make the best of it.

KATE. I'm only here till my family come.

JOHN. They won't come. They got what they wanted. Oh there'll be talk, plenty of talk of the grand dream of them taking the whole island. And maybe some night you'll be summoned by a quiet knock and hear the whisper of promises and they'll beg a meal or money off you and you'll never see them again. Forget all that, Kate.

KATE. You're bound to say that to me. I have their promise.

JOHN. A promise is just words, Kate. They're still fighting but it's

each other now. They won't come up here to face twenty
thousand guns with an Empire behind them. And that's a fact.
You are left here.

KATE. Then I am betrayed.

JOHN. Maybe you got the best of it. Think of it that way.

*Silence. He doesn't want to force her. She is not sure of him or what to
do.*

You're a lovely woman. Any man would be proud to have you.
Sit down. We'll take a drink.

He pours for them. She won't move.

It's you and me. Now. We'll go to bed.

KATE. Not now. Give me time.

He moves to her. Takes hold of her.

Don't be afeared. We're not real strangers.

KATE. Please, no.

JOHN. You smell like the spring wind.

KATE. Please. Not now.

JOHN. When would the time be? Give me a time.

KATE. I can't.

JOHN. I have to know you are mine.

KATE. Then I am lost.

JOHN. I have to have your obedience. Honour and obey. Those
are the words.

KATE. You can't impose them on me.

JOHN. Why do you make this so hard?

KATE. Why don't you understand me?

JOHN. It's not fair, woman.

KATE. I am not yours.

JOHN. You are. You have to be. And there's an end to it. You have
to accept me.

KATE. Then we are both lost.

*He lifts her up, spins her round, swings her onto the table on her back
with her head towards the audience. He is upstage of the table. Flings
up her skirts, rips away her pants, fumbles and unbuttons and thrusts*

*into her. She stays limp and as lifeless as possible through it. Her head
hanging back down off the table, the sacrifice on the wooden altar. It is
a painful business for both. The reality is not pleasure but power. When
he comes he cries out in rage and shame. Stands back, buttons. She gets
up and walks out. Left alone he lifts his hand to touch his face. It
leaves a stain of blood. He becomes aware of it on his hand. He smears
it down his face. He goes off. Bright light. New day.* VICTOR *his
younger brother, comes on in working clothes. A harder darker version of*
JOHN. *Looks around.* JOHN *comes on drying his face on a towel.
Hurries into boots and jacket.*

VICTOR Are you right?

JOHN. Aye.

VICTOR. You don't look it.

> KATE *comes on. Ignores them. Tidies things away.* VICTOR *watching
> her.* JOHN *not looking.*

JOHN. I'm away off to work.

> *She doesn't answer.*

VICTOR. Your husband's speaking to you.

> *She doesn't look at him.*

JOHN. This is Victor, my brother. Say hello to him.

> *She only looks at* VICTOR.

Come on.

> *He goes off.* VICTOR *lingers.*

VICTOR. Kate, isn't it? Kate. You'll be looking after me as well as
him. He can be too soft. But I'm hard. You mind yourself and
you'll be seen to.

> *He goes off. She fetches a box. Rescues the pieces of her flag and puts
> them and her prayer book in it. Arranges the box on some low shelves.
> Her private and personal space. Her mother,* MARY, *comes to the border
> side.*

MARY. Are you there? I won't come in. I thought I'd wait till your
man was gone. How are you?

KATE. You never told me.

MARY. It's not something to talk about.

KATE. You never told me what was going to happen.

MARY. You've lived round farmyards all your life.

KATE. I don't mean fucking.

MARY. Bless us and save us, hush your mouth.

KATE. I mean being fucked.

MARY. Let nobody hear you say that.

KATE. Funny the priest up here said the same.

MARY. You never . . .

KATE. I said to him, what do I do about it, Father? Don't call it that, he said. It's a holy act of procreation within marriage. You have to do it, he says, but you don't have to enjoy it. I see, I said, so I'm fucked whichever way I turn. That shut him up.

MARY. You never said that to him.

KATE. No, I only thought the last bit.

MARY. What kind of a daughter have I reared?

KATE. One you betrayed. Take me home.

MARY *falls silent and shifty. On the other side* JOHN *comes on with the* OFFICER.

JOHN. I don't know as this division arrangement is going to work. You've left me with a right handful here.

OFFICER. Spirited, is she?

JOHN. She's all of that. I'm not sure but I might waken up dead in my bed with my throat cut.

OFFICER. You know what the Empire expects of you.

JOHN. Yes sir, a bit of peace and quiet, sir. Keep them in their place, sir, whatever way you have to.

OFFICER. Right. Now here's a piece of advice. It never fails.

JOHN. What's that, sir?

OFFICER. Think of them as horses. The whole lesson of life is in the handling of horses. Break them, make them obedient, and you have years of good service from them. Think of her as a nervous young filly. Talk to her, stroke her, gentle her, then mount her and bridle her. If she's mulish put her between the shafts of a plough till she learns. Then reward her. Remember, a tight rein but firm not harsh. Have the feel of them between your thighs, responsive to your slightest touch, and you'll have years of good riding out of her.

JOHN. Yes sir.

OFFICER. She may need a touch of the whip, just now and again. Oh yes. I've ridden all over this island in my time. I'm right behind you. Carry on.

Marches off.

JOHN. Who does he think I am? Buffalo Bill?

He goes off.

MARY. You have to make the best of it. And that includes being civil to your mother.

KATE. Then do one thing for me. You can do that much.

MARY. What?

KATE. Bring me a gun.

MARY. Murder is a mortal sin.

KATE. Then I may as well shoot myself.

MARY. But suicide is a worse sin.

KATE. Just bring it to me.

MARY. I can't . . . I'd have to talk to your father.

KATE. He's in England looking for work.

MARY. He'll be back.

KATE. He's been gone six years.

MARY. We have nothing to spare. We depend on Gabriel so don't be looking to him for help either. I don't know what has got into you at all.

KATE. Eight inches of Protestant, mother.

MARY. I can't stay another minute to listen to this. You'll be the death of me. You'll destroy your immortal soul with this sinfulness.

KATE. I know. I shouldn't tell lies. It was only six inches.

MARY. Whatever did I do to deserve this?

KATE. You left me here. Without protection.

MARY. Can you not be content?

KATE. I have no choice here. I have no rights here.

MARY. Choice? What choice have I when it all comes down to it? Independence cut a very fine figure when it came knocking on the front door but it's far too grand to step into the kitchen. But sure we have our faith. I'll bring your own priest to you. And . . . and maybe your brother will come.

She goes off. Change of light. JOHN *comes on. From behind his back he brings an egg.*

KATE. For me?

JOHN. Aye. The brown one is laying up in the field.

KATE. I'll have it for my tea. (*Putting it on table.*)

JOHN. You will? Good.

KATE. I'll bake soda bread.

JOHN. That'll be grand.

KATE. Will you fetch me buttermilk?

JOHN. I'll do that surely. I'm going to town tomorrow. Is there anything I could get you?

KATE. I want music.

JOHN. We'll have music. It'll be grand.

Relieved he goes off. VICTOR *comes in behind her startling her.*

VICTOR. Are you looking after my brother?

KATE. What's that to you?

VICTOR. You know fine what I mean. Are you looking after him?

KATE. I'm his wife.

VICTOR. Is he looking after you?

She doesn't answer. He goes out. She leans down on the egg and crushes it on the table. Goes off. Music as from a large wind up gramophone in an upright cabinet on legs that MICK *and* WILLIE *carry on.* MICK *wipes up the egg as* WILLIE *changes the record over.* JOHN *comes on.* VICTOR *follows. The music brings* KATE. *She is delighted with it. Fetches bottle and glasses and serves them.* MICK *and* WILLIE *go off.* JOHN *offers to dance with her. She accepts even laughs as she twirls.* JOHN *is clumsy but exuberant. Making her laugh..Then* VICTOR *takes over. A better dancer but grabbing her too close. Whirls her away from the table where* JOHN *is happily drinking.* VICTOR *close to her.*

VICTOR. If you're the servant in this house shouldn't you be serving all of us? I wonder is one man enough for you.

She turns her head and pulls their joined hands over and sinks her teeth in his hand. He dare not show the pain. They dance a moment like that then she lets go and goes back to JOHN. *Lifts him to dance.* JOHN *plays the fool with his clumsiness, making her laugh.* VICTOR *watches then goes off.*

JOHN. I don't believe I'm dancing with you.

KATE. I wouldn't call it dancing.

JOHN. It'll do me. Will it do you?

KATE. It might.

JOHN. I'm sorry. I was wrong to you. In the beginning. Can you forgive me?

KATE. I might.

They dance off. The music ends. Night time. GABRIEL *appears at the border side.*

GABRIEL (*calling*). Kate? Kate, are you there, Kate?

She comes on in nightdress and gown. Sees him, runs and flings herself on him in a fierce embrace.

KATE. Gabriel, you've come for me. I knew you would. I waited and waited but I knew you'd come for me.

He's trying to disentangle himself.

GABRIEL. Kate, will you get off me.

KATE. I'd given up hope.

GABRIEL. Is your man asleep?

KATE. Nothing wakens him. Oh I dreamed of this day. That you'd come.

GABRIEL. Aye well . . . is there a drink in the house?

She rushes for bottle and glass.

Jesus but it's a cold night. (*Drinks.*) Give us another. (*She refills the glass.*) Have you anything to eat?

She gets bread and cheese for him. He wolfs it down.

That's grand, I needed that.

She is waiting but he says nothing.

KATE. Well . . . when do we go?

GABRIEL. What?

KATE. It'll only take me a minute or two to be ready.

GABRIEL. Kate . . .

KATE. We are going. That's why you've come. I knew you would keep your promise. You would come and rescue me. That's why you've come, isn't it?

GABRIEL. Me Ma sent me.

KATE. How is she?

GABRIEL. She was wondering could you spare a few bob now you're doing all right.

KATE. And is that why you are here?

GABRIEL. I came to see you. It was her wanted the money.

KATE. The monstrous oul bitch.

GABRIEL. There's a lot of mouths to feed.

KATE. So I am left here.

GABRIEL. Only for the time. Another drink would go down well.

KATE. Take it yourself.

GABRIEL (*he does*). There are moves, Kate. It's still unfinished business. The North. It is still the dream. One island.

KATE. Words, always words. But no action.

GABRIEL. That's up to you.

KATE. Me? How?

GABRIEL. If you stay here.

KATE. I don't want to stay here.

GABRIEL. We can only snipe at them over the border but you live here. You're the best placed of all of us. It's your fight. I can only help you.

KATE. I believed you. I believed you and your promises. But you're here looking for a free drink and a hand out. Just like he said. I have been dreaming.

GABRIEL. What the hell are you talking about? I've been on a job. I needed a safe stop. Whatever I'm doing I'm doing for you. But you have to stay here.

KATE. Why?

GABRIEL. If we force them out who inherits? You. The wife.

KATE. Do you want me to betray my husband?

GABRIEL. We're your true family. When the time comes will you be ready?

KATE. Is there no other way?

GABRIEL. It's what you want. Isn't it?

KATE. Is it?

GABRIEL. Our time will come. Now I better go.

KATE. Gabriel . . .

GABRIEL. You wouldn't have a few bob to spare, would you? I have to face the Ma.

She gets some from her box.

You're a darling. I'll be back.

Kisses her and goes off. She clears away. Thinking. Goes off. Light change. VICTOR *comes on with two large parcels. One long and narrow, one square and fat. Puts them on the table.* JOHN *comes out.*

VICTOR. They've come. I'll be by for you later.

He goes out. JOHN *examines the parcels. Then begins to unwrap the fat one. Satisfied with what he sees inside he begins to undress.* KATE *comes on.*

KATE. What's this?

JOHN. Will you give me a hand here?

Handing her his discarded clothes. Gets down to his long johns. She can't quite see what's in the parcel.

KATE. Are those not coming off as well?

JOHN. You know fine I sleep in them.

KATE. I was hoping for a show.

JOHN. Give over.

KATE. I'm going to buy you a nightshirt.

JOHN. I'd be cold.

KATE. With me beside you?

JOHN. I'll say this for you, you've got the beating of a hot water bottle.

KATE. Is that all I am to you?

JOHN. I don't know how I lived without you. Here, will you help me with this?

KATE. What is it?

JOHN. My uniform.

He has opened up the parcel and spreads out the jacket and trousers of a B Special uniform.

KATE. Why can't you and me just stay here being warm together? The world is outside and the door is shut.

JOHN. The world is on my back. To do my share of duty. Give us here.

Steps into the trousers. Hitches up the braces. She steps up close to him as he begins to button his fly.

KATE. Do you have to go?

JOHN. Woman dear, you have a wicked touch.

She's standing really close to him so we can't see her hands.

KATE. Is the bird taking wing?

JOHN. It's soaring. And swooping.

As he brings his hand up under her skirt.

KATE. Flying.

JOHN. Free as air.

KATE. Free.

JOHN. On the edge of the world.

KATE. Free of it.

JOHN. Soaring.

As they strain against each other he reaches back among his clothes on the table and fetches out a condom and gives it to her as they still kiss and nuzzle and hold each other. She opens it and hidden in the closeness between them slips it on him. And that's enough to make him come.

JOHN. Aaahhh.

KATE. You're in my hands, Johnny, stay in my hands, stay with me.

JOHN (*subsiding*). Aaahh.

KATE. Stay with me.

JOHN. They'll never part us. I promise you.

KATE. Don't leave me ncw.

JOHN. They'll be here for me. I have to go out on patrol.

She steps back from him, the used condom closed in her hand. He scrambles into the shirt and jacket.

KATE. What have you become? What does this make you?

JOHN. I'm a B Special. It's part time militia.

KATE. A local army?

JOHN. It's a bit of extra money.

KATE. We don't need it.

JOHN. I have to join. Everybody has joined. There's been attacks over the border. We have to defend our homes and families.

KATE. Why must you join?

JOHN. There's not much choice in it.

KATE. And what's this?

She indicates the long bundle.

JOHN. The final piece.

He rips the paper away to reveal a new rifle.

JOHN. Isn't that a fine weapon?

KATE. Is it yours now?

JOHN. Oh aye. It'll stay in the house. I have the right to keep it at all times. We'll be well defended. I hope I never have to use it.

KATE. It would be against our own people. You can't do that.

JOHN. It's only for defence. Nothing else. Here, hold it while I finish dressing.

Thrusts it at her. She doesn't want to hold it but has to. Holds it, turns it in her hands. It ends up pointing at him. He notices. Reaches and pushes the barrel aside.

JOHN. The first rule. Never point it at anyone unless you mean to use it. Here, give me.

He is now the complete picture. Uniform and rifle.

How do I look?

KATE. I don't know you.

JOHN. It's only me.

KATE. No. It is not you.

JOHN. Don't be daft.

KATE. I tell you for your own good. I do not know you. All I see is a man who is dressed to kill.

JOHN. Give over.

KATE. The men you hunt won't see you. They won't see a neighbour. They'll only see a uniform.

JOHN. You can be very strange sometimes. I'm only on patrol to keep the peace.

KATE. Don't go out. It's not our fight.

JOHN. It's every man's fight here, Kate.

KATE. I don't want it to be mine anymore. I just want you.

JOHN. It's only clothes.

KATE. Don't go.

JOHN. I have no choice.

KATE. There must be a choice. I'm making a choice. Why can't you?

VICTOR comes in also in uniform with rifle.

VICTOR. It's time to go.

KATE. John.

VICTOR. Are you right?

JOHN. Aye. I'm ready.

VICTOR. Come on then. (JOHN *doesn't move.*) Come on.

JOHN. I'll be back late.

KATE. I'll be here. Where else could I go?

JOHN. I'm off then.

VICTOR. Come on. She knows her place. She should be grateful for it. We've got a job to do.

They go off. She is left. She uncrumples her fingers and tosses down on the table the used little rubber. The PRIEST appears at the border side.

PRIEST. Are you in, daughter?

KATE (*surprised*). Father?

PRIEST. May I come in?

KATE. Yes, I'm sorry, I forget my manners. Do come in.

PRIEST. I was hoping to find you alone.

KATE. Sit down. Will you have a cup of tea?

PRIEST. It's a very cold night.

KATE. A glass of whiskey.

PRIEST. Only if you insist. (*As she pours.*) Your mother asked me to come and have a wee chat. She's worried about you.

KATE. She's worried I might come back to her.

PRIEST. Is there something troubling you?

KATE. You could say that. (*Pouring herself a drink.*)

PRIEST. Is it a domestic problem?

KATE. I've been thinking.

PRIEST. Ah. Then you'll have realised.

KATE. What?

PRIEST. That it's very bad for you. It can cause all manner of ills. It can ruin the health entirely.

KATE. Oh, you think so?

PRIEST. I know so. Leave it to those who know how to handle it.

KATE. And who might they be?

PRIEST. Your Father . . .

KATE. Is that a fact?

PRIEST. . . . . your spiritual Fathers. Only they are able to argue out the true meaning of things. It is all in the teachings of the Church. We have only to accept and believe.

KATE. Then answer me this, Father. What am I doing here? Why do I have to be here?

PRIEST. That is the question I thought you would ask me, that is the question I have come to answer.

KATE. So what is the answer?

PRIEST. You have been chosen.

KATE. Who by?

PRIEST. By God. Isn't that the most wonderful thing? That you have been chosen. It is all part of God's great plan. He has a task and a purpose for each one of us but you, you have been specially blessed.

KATE. I have?

PRIEST. And it is because you are here that God so wants and needs you to do his holy work. Isn't that a grand thing?

KATE. What work?

PRIEST. To keep the flame alight. To keep the faith of our church. Where else is our faith more despised and tested than here? Where else is there more need to fight the good fight until we have one free and holy island? It may be a long and difficult struggle. You may have to make a great sacrifice but that will only show how God loves you. Now doesn't that answer your question?

KATE. No.

PRIEST. You have only to obey, to follow the will of God. Your reward will be in heaven.

KATE. It's here, now, that troubles me. We are just two people, John and me. I think I can love him with all his faults. He says himself, it is our home and nobody else's and we must live together. I think we can live together. But will we be left alone? Or do I have to submit my dreams to his? Become a servant of his Empire? Betray my own belief? Don't tell me it's simple, father.

PRIEST. Amn't I glad you told me all this? You have been troubled. But don't worry yourself. God moves in mysterious ways his wonders to perform. You only have to take the long view. God doesn't want to come between you and your husband. All is lawful and legitimate between you. But you'll have many bonny children, a young woman like you, with hips like yours, and you will see that they grow up in our faith and sure in the fullness of time there will be more of us than there is of them and this place will be yours. It will be ours. For in the end all belongs to God. We will have an island where our church will have its proper place, as the father and teacher of all the people, with only those laws that accord with the teaching of the holy father. A holy island. Isn't that a wonderful vision?

KATE. It'll suit my mother.

PRIEST. And what finer example. Now, you will keep the faith and we will talk no more about it. Is there a drop more in the bottle?

KATE. Help yourself, father.

He reaches for the bottle and sees on the table the used condom. Picks it up with extreme distaste.

PRIEST. What is this?

KATE. Oh I'm sorry I shouldn't have left it . . .

PRIEST. What is it doing here?

KATE. I was using it.

PRIEST. You? Then whose . . . whose manly essence is in here?

KATE. My husband's. Who else?

PRIEST. I see. So he forced this on you.

KATE. No. I put it on him.

PRIEST. God save us.

KATE. I don't want to be having children yet.

PRIEST. What in the name of heaven do you want?

KATE. To be in charge of my own life. I have to be sure. Once I have a child I'm stuck here.

PRIEST. Thinking. This is what comes of thinking. On your knees. On your knees and beg God for his forgiveness. Thoughts lead to acts and acts lead to sin and sin leads to eternal damnation and that is why you must repent your thoughts. On your knees. Now.

KATE. No. This is between my husband and myself.

PRIEST. Then he has forced them on you. It is no more than one would expect. Are there any more of these?

KATE. Yes.

PRIEST. If he demands to use them put a pin hole in them.

KATE. How can I when there's a prick in there already?

PRIEST. I must pray for you. You are being corrupted by heathen ways. Remember the mission God has chosen for you. Pray. Keep the faith. It is God's will we serve, not man's.

He rushes off (taking the condom with him). She pours a drink and gulps it down. JOHN *clumps back in his uniform and gun. She goes to him. Hugs him.*

KATE. Hold me. I'm scared.

JOHN. Why would you be? We're safe here..

KATE. But . . .

Sees VICTOR *stepping in behind him and shuts up.*

JOHN. Get the two of us a drink, will you?

She grabs up the PRIEST*'s glass and puts it away. Pours for them and leaves the bottle as they slump down, tired.*

KATE. Will you be long?

JOHN. I'll be up soon.

KATE. All right. (*To* VICTOR.) Goodnight.

VICTOR. Goodnight.

She goes off.

VICTOR. Is she fit?

JOHN. I'm a lucky man and that's a fact.

VICTOR. Any sign of a baby yet?

JOHN. In good time.

VICTOR. People will begin to wonder.

JOHN. Wonder what?

VICTOR. Is she feeding you.

JOHN. Let them. God, it was cold out there tonight. Quiet though.

VICTOR. I'd like to get my hands on a few of them. You need sons to grow up and defend this place.

JOHN. Aye.

VICTOR. You make sure you bring them up right.

JOHN. That's her job.

VICTOR. We took our lead from our father.

JOHN. Aye, look what it got us.

VICTOR. It got us our own country. Would you want to live in the south?

JOHN. No, but they're people just like us.

VICTOR. She's turning your head.

JOHN. They're our neighbours.

VICTOR. They're our enemy. They won't rest till they steal it off us.

JOHN. We won't always be fighting.

VICTOR. What if something happens to you?

JOHN. Nothing's going to happen to me.

VICTOR. I wouldn't inherit. She would. She and her family. Think about that.

JOHN. Nothing's going to happen to me.

VICTOR. You're too damn trusting for your own good. You're giving them one hell of an opportunity.

JOHN. I'm going to bed. (*Gets up.*)

VICTOR. What do I do if anything happens to you?

JOHN. Do what's right.

VICTOR. How do you know you can trust her?

JOHN. I won't have that kind of talk in this house.

VICTOR. But how can you be sure of her?

JOHN. Because I love her.

VICTOR. This is land we're talking about, John. Not love. Land. Our land. You took an oath when you put on that uniform.

JOHN. I'll honour it.

VICTOR. An oath to defend this place. You should be keeping her in her place. Where she belongs. Flat on her back having good loyal sons. If you don't, I will.

JOHN. Do what?

VICTOR. Defend this land. It's mine too. Brother.

JOHN. You should get married yourself. Brother.

VICTOR. I'll take my pick in my own good time.

JOHN. It's more a matter of who'd have you. Drink up. A toast. To the future. It can only get better for sure it can't get worse.

They touch glasses and drink. VICTOR *takes his gun and goes.*

VICTOR. I'll see you.

JOHN *takes off jacket.* KATE *comes back. He hugs her.*

JOHN. What had you troubled before?

KATE. It's nothing.

JOHN. Nothing will harm us here. I got a new box of them johnnies.

KATE. Maybe we shouldn't bother with them.

JOHN. Kate.

KATE. Well, what are you waiting for? Just think, you can do it with your socks off.

They embrace. Go off. Music swells then into a bright tempo as the lights brighten for dawn and KATE *comes out, stretching and smiling, to greet the light. Happy. Until* GABRIEL *appears from hiding on the border side. Obviously been out all night.*

KATE. Who's there? Who's out there? Gabriel. What are you doing here. It's not safe for you. Away home before they see you.

GABRIEL. I made a promise to you.

KATE. I don't hold you to that anymore. I'm past that now. Go home, Gabriel.

GABRIEL. Don't you want this place? You have a right to it.

KATE. I have what I want. I have enough.

GABRIEL. That's not my sister talking. I always looked up to you, Kate, because you would stand up for yourself. You would take no messing. Where are they patrolling these nights, Kate?

KATE. You let my husband be.

GABRIEL. It's not him we have to worry about. It's his brother. There'll be no dealing with him.

KATE. Go home, Gabriel.

GABRIEL. It's better you know nothing.

KATE. There should be nothing to know.

GABRIEL. A promise is a promise. You leave it to me.

KATE. I don't hold you to that promise.

GABRIEL. It was a promise made to history.

KATE. What does that mean?

GABRIEL. It means everything.

KATE. Go home. It's me that has to live here. Go on, away.

She shooes him off. Turns back to the house. Light darkens. Music underscores her change of mood. JOHN *comes on in uniform.*

KATE. Do you have to go?

JOHN. We're on stand-by all the time now.

KATE. I don't want you to go.

JOHN. There's been a lot of raids.

KATE. Please, don't go out tonight.

JOHN. I have to.

KATE. Please.

JOHN. Don't make it hard.

KATE. I don't want either of us to be part of it. We have each other. Nobody else matters. That's the only way we will survive. Let's stay in here together.

JOHN. You be warm for me coming home. I'll be all right.

KATE. Say you love me.

JOHN. You know I do.

KATE. Say it.

JOHN. I love you.

KATE. I love you. Isn't that enough?

JOHN. I wish it was.

KATE. Don't go. I have a fear for you.

JOHN. It's all for show. Acting the big fella. They'll soon give up.
They don't really want us. Sure what would they do with us all?
We'd just mess up their nice new state. They may claim the
whole island but the north has always been different. We'd be
more trouble than we're worth.

KATE. Then there's no need for you to go.

JOHN. They won't go away if we don't stand up to them. Will you
quit fussing now? I'm off.

KATE. Don't you understand my fear?

JOHN. No, I don't. But then you're a woman and sometimes you're
away with the fairies. And I love you for it. I'll be back as soon as
I can.

*He goes off. She sits staring into space as it darkens. GABRIEL comes
at a scrambling gasping run from non border side. Tumbles in and
falls panting.*

KATE. What has happened? Gabriel, what's been done? Are you all
right?

He reaches inside his jacket. Gives her a gun.

GABRIEL. Here, take this, hide it for me. Keep it. You said you
wanted one. Give us a drink.

She reaches the bottle. He slugs from it, revives, gets up.

I'm away. Not a word. I'll be back sometime. There's been great
deeds tonight.

*He runs off. She is left with gun. Shocked. Rouses herself and hides it in
her box. As she turns at a rush come WILLIE and MICK carrying the
body of JOHN on a stretcher. They lay him the length of the table then
fall back. VICTOR walks on. KATE goes to the table. Touches JOHN's
face.*

VICTOR. It was an ambush. He was in front. He was the only one
hit. It's bad deeds tonight.

Staring at her. She moves to put the body of JOHN between them.

What do you know of this? What do you know of this?

KATE. Nothing.

VICTOR. Are you sure?

KATE. Yes.

VICTOR. I'm sure he was picked out.

KATE. Surely not.

VICTOR. My big brother. He paid the great sacrifice. It won't be in vain. Will it? Will it?

KATE. No.

VICTOR. Have you got what you wanted here?

KATE. No.

VICTOR. I suppose you want the place now.

KATE. No.

VICTOR. Then what do you want?

KATE. I want what I can't have.

VICTOR. What?

KATE. My man back.

VICTOR. Do you?

> *Grabbing her and pulling her bent across the body. His face close to hers. Both half demented.*

I think you wanted what he had.

KATE. No.

VICTOR. Then what do you want here?

KATE. I want . . .

VICTOR. What?

KATE. Whatever John wanted. Leave me with him!

VICTOR. He wanted me to have it.

> *She tries to pull away.*

I'm taking it. It's my house now. My inheritance. All of it. And you are part of it. You will stay with me and make no claim on it.

> *She pulls away from him, turns towards the box. He comes round to cut her off. She's trapped behind the table.*

There's nowhere to go. You live here. It's you and me for it now.

> *She hits out at him.*

This place is mine and everything that's in it. That's how it has to be. He won't die in vain. You'll pay for him.

He grabs her, flings her forward across the body, her face towards the audience. He is behind her. Throws up her skirts. Behind the bunched cloth unbuttons and thrusts into her. (Not an act of sodomy.) Quick. Harsh. Comes with a manic cry. Turns away from her. Goes off. She lies across the body.

KATE. I can feel a child in me. I want a son. I want a strong son to grow up and free me. I put a curse on this divided house. A curse that will not lift till my strong son tears it tumbling down upon his father's roaring head. And saves me.

WILLIE and MICK come forward and lift her tenderly up. Dab at her tears. They lead her off.

ACT TWO

The house. WILLIE *and* MICK *carry on a large box draped in a red cloth and set it on the table.*

WILLIE. You see . . . what bothers me about Isaac . . .

MICK. You're not starting up about that again.

WILLIE. It bothers me.

MICK. Is there nothing else you and I can argue about?

WILLIE. Like what?

MICK. Like . . . oh I don't know. I don't know why we're still worrying away about how we got into this mess.

WILLIE. You see the problem wih Isaac . . .

MICK. The problem for Isaac is that he is tied down like a parcel. He can't move. He has no choice.

WILLIE. You always have a choice.

MICK. Ah don't give me all that crap about free will. It's fine in theory but it means bugger all in practice. He's stuck.

WILLIE. He can still think for himself.

MICK. Think? What help is that? Round and round in the same circles. I did enough thinking. In the end you just get on with things and take what's coming to you.

WILLIE. There has to be more to it than that.

There is a groaning cry.

MICK. What's that?

The cries continue. They look for the source of them. They come from under the cloth.

BOYD (*crying out*). Aaah . . . aaah . . . I can't . . . I'm stuck . . . I'm stuck . . . I'm stuck . . . aaah . . . I can't . . .

They stand over the cloth, look nervously at each other, decide to pull cloth away. Reveals a naked young man lying curled up in the foetal position with his head bent tightly inwards and down on his chest, trying with all his strength to force his head up to free himself. (Same actor who played JOHN.)

I can't move my head . . . my neck . . . my neck . . . oh the pain on my neck . . . the force on my neck . . . aaah . . . my neck . . .

They are on either side viewing his struggle.

WILLIE. He's stuck.

MICK. I can see that.

WILLIE. We have to help him.

MICK. How?

WILLIE. We've got to.

BOYD. Ah . . . ah . . . I'm stuck . . . my neck . . .

WILLIE. We have to help him.

MICK. How? You can't get in there with him and give him a bunk up.

WILLIE. Push, come on, lad, push, come on, push.

BOYD. I'm trying . . .

WILLIE. Push. At least give him a bit of encouragement. Come on now . . .

BOYD. I want to move . . . I want to come out . . . I'm being pushed to come out . . .

MICK. That's right, come on.

BOYD. I'm being pushed but I'm being held back . . . I can't . . . My neck . . . oh the pain in my neck . . .

WILLIE. He's in trouble. Come on, lad, push now, push now, push now, push . . .

MICK. He's not a frigging train. He has to let it happen.

BOYD. I can't . . . I can't . . .

WILLIE. He has to help himself: Come on, now push . . .

BOYD. I want to come out but it won't let me . . .

WILLIE. Don't give up now.

MICK. He's helpless. He'll just get whatever's coming to him.

WILLIE. He can bloody well help himself. Come on now, another big effort . . . push . . .

BOYD. Ah . . . ah . . . ah . . . (*Renewed effort.*) the pain . . . the pain on my neck . . .

Neck bent even further in as his body convulses pushing on it.

I want to come out . . . I'm being pushed to come out . . . I'm being held back from coming out . . . let me out . . . What do you want from me? . . . Ah . . . Ah . . .

WILLIE. Come on, boy, come on. Want it . . . want it . . .

BOYD. Aaaaaghhh . . .

And his head comes up free and his body flops loose.

WILLIE. He did it.

BOYD *opens his eyes. Looks.*

BOYD. The light. The light. The light is wonderful.

WILLIE. He did it.

MICK. Nature did it.

WILLIE. He got himself free. You saw it.

MICK. He was given his life. That's not the same thing at all.

BOYD *is gasping air through his mouth, experimental.*

BOYD. I can breathe. I can breathe. It's wonderful. I can breathe. The light. Oh the light. Um Um Um Um . . .

He makes sucking noises.

WILLIE. What's up with him now?

MICK. He wants a tit.

WILLIE. Well, don't look at me.

BOYD. Um Um Um . . . ahhh . . . (*Crying for food.*)

WILLIE. What do we do? What do we give him?

They look round wildly.

MICK. Give him your thumb till I find something.

He rushes to search for a bottle. WILLIE *sticks his thumb in the boy's mouth.* BOYD *sucks hard. Stops breathing.*

WILLIE. Let go . . . let go . . . Jesus. Mick, he's going purple here . . . he's not breathing . . .

MICK. Get your thumb out.

WILLIE. I can't. He's got a suck like a heifer.

Then the boy begins to breathe convulsively through his nose as he sucks, and WILLIE *laughs in relief.*

That's it. That's right, you've got a nose. You didn't know you had a nose, did you? That's it. You breathe through your nose if your mouth's full. It's easy, isn't it? You don't have to panic.

BOYD *has experimented all he can with a thumb and now rejects it. Sets up a cry for food.*

Mick, will you hurry up, he's crying. Don't cry now. What do I do? Mick, will you hurry up.

MICK *has filled a bottle with milk and got the teat on. Rushes back. Gives it to boy. He sucks up milk. They sit back beaming.*

MICK. There now, get that down you.

WILLIE. He's going at that well. There's nothing to it, is there. His neck looks all right. What do you think?

MICK. Aye, he's straight enough.

WILLIE. He's a big strong lad. I told you he'd do it.

BOYD *flings the bottle away with a terrible cry.*

WILLIE. What's up now?

BOYD. It's the wrong smell. It's the wrong smell. Aaagh.

WILLIE. What the hell did you give him?

MICK. Milk. (*Rescuing bottle.*)

WILLIE. See what you've done to him.

MICK. What I did to him?

BOYD. I want my mother. I want my mother.

WILLIE. What do we tell him?

BOYD. Maaaaaaah.

MICK. She's not well, lad, she's sick, it was a hard birth.

WILLIE. She'll come, she'll come, she'll find you.

BOYD. I wanted to come out but I was forced out. Don't stop touching me. Don't put me down. Don't leave me. I don't know where I am.

He gives a great cry of anger and frustration and sorrow for himself. They crouch by him, touching him.

MICK. Welcome to the world, boy.

WILLIE. There now.

Door opens. BOYD *calms but whimpers now.* VICTOR *comes on.* WILLIE *and* MICK *fall back.* VICTOR *goes up to the boy and looks closely at him, staring into his face.* BOYD *reaches towards him.* VICTOR *ignores it. Goes out.*

WILLIE. Who do you think he looks like?

MICK. Now there's a question.

WILLIE. Jesus, I'm knackered. I don't know how women do it. I'm glad I'm a man.

MICK. Are you sure it's better?

WILLIE. If it means having the like of you jumping on me I'll stick to being a fella.

BOYD *has calmed down and has now begun to explore himself. Open and closes his fingers. Move his limbs, feel his face. They watch him. As lights change, he becomes more physically assured but a baby. Eventually finds his penis. Holds it, examines it.* WILLIE *goes and gets a top and pants, like a sweat suit or romper suit. Throws them to him.*

WILLIE. Here. Cover yourself. Your troubles are only starting.

BOYD *slowly dresses. Then sits and sucks his thumb.*

WILLIE *and* MICK *fade off as* VICTOR *comes on.* BOYD *lifts up his arms towards him.*

BOYD. Dada . . . dada . . .

VICTOR. Aye. You're mine. I have a son.

KATE *comes on. Looking haggard, beaten down.* BOYD *turns towards her but she hangs back. Until* VICTOR *nods.*

Go on. Look after him.

She goes and gets down with the boy and cuddles him.

KATE. He looks a lot like you.

VICTOR. I looked a lot like my brother.

KATE. He'll be a good son. Won't you? You'll be a good son for your Dada and Mama.

BOYD (*new sound*). Ma Ma . . .

KATE. Yes you will. And you'll grow up strong. You'll grow up strong for your Mama.

BOYD. Mama . . . Mama . . .

VICTOR. We have to name him.

KATE. I want to call him Patrick.

VICTOR. That's no name for him.

KATE. He has to have a name. He has to be baptised.

VICTOR. He will be. As my son.

KATE. I have a right. I have a right to have him baptised in my own faith. It goes with the mother. That's my right.

VICTOR. He's mine.

KATE. You can't take him away from me.

Holds boy close. He is uneasy.

BOYD. Dada . . . Dada . . .

VICTOR. Is he not mine?

KATE. Why do you ask that?

VICTOR. It doesn't matter. I'm the only father he'll ever have. Give him over to me.

KATE. No.

VICTOR. Then I'll drown him.

KATE. No.

VICTOR. Only a son of my own seed will ever inherit this house. Now. Is he not mine?

KATE. I could kill you.

VICTOR. I'm sure you could. Give him to me.

KATE. What are you going to do with him?

VICTOR. Come up here, son.

Takes the boy by the arm and stands him up.

BOYD. Mama . . . Mama . . .

KATE. Don't harm him.

VICTOR *puts a hand on the boy's head.*

VICTOR. My mother's maiden name was Boyd. She gave that to me as my middle name. I give it to you. I name you Boyd. And now you know what family you come from.

BOYD. Mama . . . Mama . . .

Tries to get out from VICTOR's hand and turn to her. VICTOR slaps him.

VICTOR. What do you say. What do you say?

BOYD. Da. Da. Da.

VICTOR. I name you for my own.

BOYD. Da. Da.

> VICTOR *walks out.* KATE *gets up and puts her arms around the* BOY *who is standing rigid, not crying.*

KATE. It's all right, son, it's all right.

BOYD. Da. Da. Da.

KATE. You're my own, my little Paddywhack. That'll be our secret name. You'll grow up strong for your Mama.

BOYD. Mama . . . Mama . . .

KATE. Oh I'll never leave you. I'll never abandon you. Now, hush, now, hush. You lie down. There's a good boy. You lie down and go to sleep. Sleep so you can grow up a big man for your Mama. There, there now.

> *He stretches out and she covers him, singing quietly to him. He sleeps. She sits by him. It darkens.* VICTOR *is framed by the inside light, big in his uniform and rifle. Looks at them. Goes out. She moves away from* BOYD *but watches to be sure he sleeps. Sits at the table. At the border side comes* GABRIEL.

GABRIEL. Kate. Kate.

KATE. Who is it? Come out where I can see you.

GABRIEL. Is it safe?

KATE. Gabriel? Come in here.

> *He comes slowly in. She flies at him, attacking him, battering.*

You killed him. You killed my husband. You killed my John.

GABRIEL. I wasn't to know. I didn't know. Will you stop?

KATE. Why did you have to do it? Why? Why my John?

GABRIEL (*grabbing her arms*). Will you stop now?

KATE. Why him?

GABRIEL. All I saw was a uniform. I shot at a uniform. A uniform with a man in it. That was my aim. That's all I saw. It didn't matter who the man was if he was in a uniform.

KATE. Damn the day he put it on.

GABRIEL. Will you calm down? Let go now.

She steps away. He takes a deep breath. She sits again.

Kate, if I'd known . . .

KATE. You'd still have done it.

GABRIEL. But it was his own fault.

KATE. His fault?

GABRIEL. He should never have put on the uniform. You said it yourself. He gave up being his own man.

KATE. Were you wearing a uniform?

GABRIEL. I took an oath to the secret army. Look, I came to say I'm sorry. And I am sorry. And I came. I didn't dodge it. I'm sorry. I owed it to you to come.

KATE. Aye.

GABRIEL. I hoped you would forgive me. Can you at least understand?

KATE. I understand.

GABRIEL. And I came to say thank you.

KATE. Thank me? Thank me for what?

GABRIEL. For helping me. For helping me get away and telling them nothing.

KATE. Is that what I did? I suppose it was. I didn't think.

GABRIEL. Do they suspect you?

KATE. No. No.

GABRIEL. I'll make it up to you.

KATE. How? How can you repay the death of a husband?

GABRIEL. By taking over this house for you. So you can know he didn't die in vain.

KATE. By more deaths?

GABRIEL. If it has to be.

KATE. I should throw you out.

GABRIEL. Then you lose everything. You weren't given the chance to inherit this place, were you? Victor took it. When it was rightfully yours. They'll never give it up unless we take it. Is this the boy?

KATE. Aye.

GABRIEL (*looking at the child*). What do you want him to grow up to inherit? What's his future going to be?

KATE. Mine.

GABRIEL. Then help me.

KATE. How could it be done?

GABRIEL. I'll think about that one. Victor's a different class of a proposition. I won't risk staying any longer. I'll come back.

KATE. How's my mother?

GABRIEL. She wants to come and see you but she was afraid. She made me come.

KATE. She shouldn't have had to. It was the least you could do for me.

GABRIEL. I came, didn't I? It's risky work, Kate.

KATE. Do you want the gun? I've kept it hidden.

GABRIEL. Aye.

She goves over to the box, GABRIEL *with her. Unseen by them* BOYD *wakens and sits up a little to watch as she gets the hidden gun out.*

KATE. Here. Away you go before you get caught here.

GABRIEL (*handing the gun back*). Listen, to be on the safe side, you keep it. I wouldn't want it on me if I was stopped. I'll get another one. I'll be back. (*Pauses as he goes.*) The boy has the look of his Da.

He goes off. She holds the gun.

BOYD. Mama . . . Mama . . .

She keeps the gun hidden away from him.

KATE. Shh, my wee Paddywhack, you go to sleep now.

Watches till his eyes close then turns to hide the gun in the box. As soon as she turns his eyes open and he watches her hide the gun. When she turns back his eyes are closed. Abruptly VICTOR *comes on.* BOYD*'s eyes open and he watches as* VICTOR *puts the rifle away and takes off his jacket, avoiding looking at* KATE. BOYD*'s eyes close as* VICTOR *turns towards him.* VICTOR *looks down at him.*

VICTOR. He'll be safe. You'll both be safe. With me. (*Looks at her.*) Are you coming to bed?

Walks off without waiting for her. She follows. When she is gone BOYD *crawls over and takes the gun out and plays with it.* MICK *comes on and gently takes the gun off him and puts it back in the box.* BOYD *starts to cry . WILLIE comes on.*

WILLIE. What are you doing to him?

MICK. Nothing.

BOYD. Mama . . . Mama . . . (*crying louder.*)

Nobody comes. Begins to really cry.

VICTOR (*off stage*). Leave him be. He has to learn.

BOYD *cries louder. MICK and WILLIE look at each other, anxious and helpless, then WILLIE rushes to the gramophone and winds it up and puts record on. BOYD still crying but intrigued as music plays. A foxtrot. WILLIE and MICK dance together for him and he stops crying and laughs at them. They take him up and join him in the dance, then as the music ends the lights brighten into morning and with some ceremony they demonstrate for him how a brush can be a pretend horse and set him riding delightedly round the room. VICTOR in his working clothes comes on, hands behind his back, a package in them.*

VICTOR. C'mere, boy.

BOYD. Daddy.

VICTOR. I've got something for you.

BOYD. A present? A present for me? Where is it, let me see it.

VICTOR. Which hand is it in?

BOYD. That one.

VICTOR *brings that hand out empty. They play that game, VICTOR switching the package behind his back until BOYD guesses right and VICTOR gives him the parcel. He unwraps it. It is a toy pistol and gunbelt western style.*

VICTOR. There, your first gun. What do you say?

BOYD. Thank you.

VICTOR. Daddy.

BOYD. Thank you, Daddy.

VICTOR. You want to be your father's son, don't you?

BOYD. Yes, Daddy.

VICTOR. Good, now, let's put this on.

Buckles the belt round him.

There. Now, let's see you draw. No, no, you have to be quicker than that. Come on now. Slap and pull. That's it. That's better. Now try this. You see now, I clap my hands together and you try and get the gun between them. You have to be fast. That's good, that's better.

As they practice this game KATE *comes on.* VICTOR *registers her disapproval.*

BOYD. Daddy, why do the Indians want to kill the cowboys?

She goes off.

VICTOR. They want the land. They want what doesn't belong to them. That's why you have to shoot them.

BOYD. Why do they want it?

VICTOR. They're nothing but ignorant heathen savages. A people that couldn't even invent the wheel for themselves. They had that whole land and didn't know what to do with it. It took the white man to come and show them what to do with it.

BOYD. And that's why we have to chase them?

VICTOR. We defend ourselves. Defend what we built. You come from good stock, boy. Your forefathers helped shaped that country. We built roads and towns and carved out farms and drained land and established law and order and ownership. But were the natives grateful? They still claim it's theirs, everything we made of it that they couldn't.

BOYD. I want to be a cowboy. The cowboys are the good guys.

VICTOR. Aye, they're the white men.

BOYD. And I'll kill all the Indians.

VICTOR. Here, give us that.

Takes the gun and puts a roll of caps in it.

These are just like bullets.

BOYD. Do the Indians believe in God?

VICTOR. No.

BOYD. What is God?

VICTOR. There is only one God. The Father, the Son, and the Holy Ghost.

BOYD. That's three.

VICTOR. They're all one. God is your conscience, boy. The other lot will tell you that God and their church has a law for everything and you have to obey it. But a man is what he makes of himself. Each man has his own truce with God and his conscience. He is responsible for himself. You remember that.

And someday we'll get you a real gun. Would you like that?

BOYD. Yes, Daddy.

VICTOR. Then you'll be your father's son. (*Hands over toy gun.*) Now. Are you ready.

Holds out his hands. BOYD *holsters gun.*

Draw!

And he claps his hands but BOYD *gets the gun between them and pulls the trigger and keeps pulling as the caps pop off.* VICTOR *falls straight backwards and lies stony still.*

BOYD. Daddy . . . Daddy . . . Da . . .

Shocked. Looks down at VICTOR *who lies still.* BOYD'*s face crumples into tears.*

Daddy . . . Daddy . . .

Gets down and shakes him. VICTOR *limp.*

Daddy, I didn't do it, I didn't mean it . . . (*Crying.*)

And VICTOR *suddenly rises up and grabs him. He howls.*

VICTOR. Now let that learn you. It's all right, boy, but let that learn you. You listen to me. You never, never, point a gun at any person unless you mean to use it. Guns kill. You can never be too careful with them. You never point a gun at anyone unless you mean it. Do you understand me? Do you understand me?

BOYD. Yes, Daddy.

VICTOR. That's just to play with but you remember. A gun is a servant and never your master. You are responsible for it not it for you. I'm glad you like your present.

He walks off. BOYD *left with gun.*

WILLIE. You see, the trouble with Isaac . . .

MICK. Ah for fuck's sake.

He walks off and WILLIE *follows.* KATE *comes on and picks up the broom. Little comedy of sweeping* BOYD *away.*

KATE. Come on, away with you till I get my work done. Come on. And take that thing off. Find something else to play with. Go on.

BOYD goes off. KATE goes on cleaning. Her mother appears at the border side.

MARY. Hello. Am I welcome?

KATE *ignores her.*

I have something for you. I brought this for you. For the boy.

KATE *comes to her.* MARY *hands her a little pot.*

KATE. What is it?

MARY. It's holy water. For the boy.

KATE. What do you want here?

MARY. I hoped I could see my grandson. And to see how my daughter is. But I won't come in.

KATE. Please yourself.

MARY. It's a grand place you have now. Your new man must be working well. We all pray for you.

KATE. Aye.

Goes and puts pot away in her box.

MARY. It's grand. Compared to the place I have to live in. It's all since that useless father of yours came home. Him and his big ideas. Sure I could only live with him when he was away over the water.

KATE. Throw him out if you can't live with him.

MARY. I'd have the priest on me. I don't see you throwing yours out.

KATE. I have my son to protect.

MARY. And so do I too. I'm worn out with worry. Isn't Gabriel the only one in work and bringing in a bit of money. But he has his father and God knows who going on at him. He's away for nights at a time and I'm too sick to sleep worrying about him. Thinking about him being tempted into some rash madness that will bring him home to me cold on a stretcher. All for listening to people who should know better. It's a mother's torment to worry about her son.

KATE. Aye.

MARY. He's better staying at home. You lost a husband, Kate, you don't want to lose a brother. Is this the boy?

As BOYD *comes on. Still wearing gunbelt.*

Isn't he a handsome lad? And so like his father. It's all God's will, Kathleen. I'll not stay. It will only make things worse. I've seen him now and who he's like. Maybe one day I'll be able to come and stay if it would be no trouble.

She hurries off.

BOYD. Who was that, Mammy?

KATE. Never mind. Can you keep a secret, my little Paddywhack?

BOYD. Yes.

KATE. It'll be our secret.

Getting out the pot of water.

BOYD. What is it? I like secrets.

KATE. Come here.

Sprinkles water on his head.

I baptise you Patrick.

BOYD. Is that it? What's the secret?

KATE. I'm just making you mine and God's.

BOYD. Why mammy?

KATE. You'll know your history in time. Now take that off you.

BOYD. Aw, mum.

KATE. Off with it. If you were to go into the pantry and look in the big tin box you might find a big slice of cake with that pink icing that you like. Go on with you. It's our secret.

BOYD. Yes, mum.

He goes off. She holds gun belt, takes out gun and weighs it in her hand, thinking.

KATE. I must be mad.

Hides the pot.

VICTOR *comes on with a mug of tea and sits to polish his boots.*

KATE. Victor?

VICTOR. What?

KATE. I'd like to go and visit my mother. (*No answer.*) Just for a day. To see how she is. (*No answer.*) And to see my brother. See my sisters.

VICTOR. On your own?

KATE. I'd have to take the boy with me.

VICTOR. No.

KATE. Why not?

VICTOR. Because I say so.

KATE. I'm asking for a reason.

VICTOR. He belongs here.

KATE. She's his grandmother.

VICTOR. I've said no.

KATE. He ought to know his history.

VICTOR. He'll know mine. That'll be enough for him.

KATE. He has to grow up his own way.

VICTOR. He will. The right way.

KATE. Victor . . .

VICTOR. I won't have him turned against me.

KATE. It's only for a day. (*No answer.*) I live here. I am trying to make the best of it here, Victor. You have to give me something. (*No answer.*) I'm not going there to ask them to do anything for me. It would be wrong of me to expect that. My place is here.

VICTOR. Aye but you don't want to be here. Do you want to be here with me?

KATE. It's not a matter of what I want. It's a matter of what's right, what's right for the boy. What's best for all of us.

VICTOR. That's not my question.

KATE. I'm saying my place is here. It's what John would have wanted.

He puts the brush down.

VICTOR. You have some cheek. How do you expect me to trust you after what happened to him?

KATE. I had no part of what happened.

VICTOR. Oh I'll grant you, you didn't pull the trigger.

KATE. I knew nothing of it.

VICTOR. You were the cause of it.

KATE. I was not. I loved him.

VICTOR. Aye, go on, stab the knife in me. Sometimes I wish you would. Come up on me sleeping and cut my throat. I know fine what you feel for me. You think you hide it but you don't. I see the way you look at me. How do you think I feel when I look at you and all I see is my brother in your eyes. It's him you think of when you suffer my love. I can love too. I can hurt too. But I won't be caught as he was caught and I won't be soft where he was soft.

KATE. I am offering . . .

VICTOR. Tell the truth. I hear it every day. I hear it in your heart.

KATE. I have tried . . .

VICTOR. Jesus, but I am tormented. Are you mine? Is this house mine? Is the boy mine? I'm sorry I can't bring John back. He was my brother too. Who's is the boy, Kate?

KATE. He's yours.

VICTOR. Tell me the truth.

KATE. He has no father.

VICTOR. I can't trust you.

KATE. You can't trust yourself because of what you've done to me.

VICTOR. I have to know. Are you just telling me what I want to hear?

KATE. Maybe I'm not.

VICTOR. What kind of an answer is that?

KATE. Do you want to trust me?

VICTOR. Yes, God help me, I do.

KATE. Do you? Or do you just want to pick at it, inflame it, nurse the worm in your gut? We have to live together. For the boy's sake. We have to find a way to live together. Do you want that?

VICTOR. Yes.

KATE. Is that because you have no choice?

VICTOR. I have no choice.

KATE. You could put me out.

VICTOR. Then we'd have to put everyone like you out.

KATE. You could do it.

VICTOR. It wouldn't be right. I just want my own house.

KATE. Then you will have to trust me if we are to live in it.

VICTOR. Make me trust you.

KATE. No. You have to earn it. You can't expect blind obedience from me. I won't give it. No matter what you do to me. Let me take the boy to see my family. It will only be for a day. We will come back.

VICTOR. No.

KATE. Why not?

VICTOR. He is mine.

KATE. Victor, you are a bloody great fool.

VICTOR. He will be mine because I will make him mine in all my likeness and beliefs and you will all be afeared to see him walk upon his land.

KATE. Victor, you are nurturing a worm that will grow into a snake that will eat you from the inside out until its gleaming eye will be the centre of your eyeball and its tongue will slither out of your mouth and poison your spit so that all the words you speak will shower out hate and you will poison your own seed. Let us go.

VICTOR. No. You want him to be John's. You want for him to know he is John's. You wish it was me in the ground and not him.

KATE. I do. But I can't have what I want and you can't either.

VICTOR. You will not step beyond the bounds of this place with that boy.

KATE. And what if I defy you?

VICTOR. Then you will have sacrificed him. We will have other children.

KATE. We cannot live like this.

VICTOR. Will you stop tormenting me? We will live the way I say.

He hits her and she falls. BOYD *has come on and sees this. Goes to move to her.*

BOYD. Mama.

VICTOR. Leave her be.

He drags the boy out. She sits up.

KATE. How many times. How many times has my mind shuddered and drawn back from the thought of death, of taking away a life. How many times have I sworn and then unsworn, repented all my bitter urges. How many times have I tipped on the brink of saying it has to be done, there is no other future. How many times said, no it will bring nothing but calamity on everyone belonging to me. How many times have I told myself to live and suffer and hope and surely in the long march of time there will be reward. How many times suppressed the answer that nothing gets better for the victim until they throw off that name and claim themselves as equal, that all change is won by some struggle or another.

She gets up.

If nothing is given it must be taken. I will not listen to my mind anymore I will listen to the tides and molten surges of my history and anger. Let them guide me. Let there be murder done.

She goes off.

BOYD *comes on, secretive, not wanting to be caught. He wears his gunbelt but without the toy gun. Sneaks to* KATE's *box and takes out the real gun. Fondles it, points it, looks down the barrel. Tries it in the holster. Tries to draw with it. It is really too heavy for him. Doesn't fire it but makes the sounds of firing. Then, scared of being caught, puts it away and goes off as* KATE *and* GABRIEL *appear outside at the border side.*

GABRIEL. I'm saying no. It can't be done.

KATE. It must.

GABRIEL. It's too bloody risky.

KATE. You did it once.

GABRIEL. I won't be that lucky a second time.

KATE. There has to be a way.

GABRIEL. Jesus, you're a typical woman, all feelings and no sense. If you'd just think about it you'd see I was right.

KATE. I see you don't want to do it.

GABRIEL. You can't catch him off his guard.

KATE. He isn't on guard in his own bed.

GABRIEL. That's crazy.

KATE. Are you afraid to do it?

GABRIEL. No. I'm just not rushing into it. I have to be sure I can get away with it.

KATE. I see.

GABRIEL. What?

KATE. If it's going to be done I'll have to do it myself.

GABRIEL. I wouldn't go back on my word, not to my own sister.

KATE. I have to be free.

GABRIEL. You don't know all that's involved.

KATE. I know you.

GABRIEL. Ah come on now.

KATE. I have carried you and cleaned your snot and wiped your arse and minded you and saved you from beatings and bought you sweeties when you cried. I brought you up, my young brother. I want your forfeit now. I hold you to your promise.

GABRIEL. Kate . . .

KATE. Should this place be ours?

GABRIEL. Yes.

KATE. Do we have to take it?

GABRIEL. Yes.

KATE. Will we have to kill for it?

GABRIEL. Well . . .

KATE. It cannot be left to another time. It must be done now.

GABRIEL. When the time is right.

KATE. Swear it, promise. Victor will die. Swear it.

GABRIEL. Well . . .

KATE. How else do we get it?

GABRIEL. I don't know. But the last time only made things worse. We don't want to rush at it.

KATE. You're afraid.

GABRIEL. And you're not wise. The only way I can see to catch him off his guard is if he was with you or the boy and that's too big a risk to take.

KATE. Then the boy can do it.

GABRIEL. Jesus, Kate . . .

KATE. He'll go anywhere for the boy. We can make him take a trip somewhere and set a trap, an ambush. The bog road. If they came back on the bog road.

GABRIEL (*grabbing her*). Kate . . . Kate . . . look at me . . .

KATE. If you won't do it I can teach the boy to use the gun . . .

GABRIEL. Kate . . . that's enough . . . you're getting beyond it

now . . . you're way past yourself . . . Kate . . . get a grip on
yourself. Kate! (*Shakes her.*)

KATE. What?

GABRIEL. Let's you and me go in and have a drink and just calm
down.

KATE. I am calm.

GABRIEL. You're not wise. Come on. (*Dragging her in.*) You need to
stop tormenting yourself.

KATE. It can be done. Then I will have my son.

He gets bottle and glasses. Pours.

GABRIEL. Sit down. Drink that. Take a slug of it. Go on. All right?

Makes sure she drinks, drinks deep himself.

Jesus, you had me scared there. You're not yourself. Look, we'll
bide our time, see how things go, all right?

Pours more drinks.

GABRIEL. It'll all look different in the morning. Here, take
another drink. Good, that'll help. (*As she drinks.*) There's other
things to talk about. It's not often I see you. The oul ma's as
bad as ever. It's the priest this and the church that. They have
every penny off her. Did I tell you I've met a girl, a nice girl,
imagine me courting . . .

KATE. You swore an oath to help me. You swore not to rest until
this whole island was ours and the foreign occupiers were gone.
You swore it.

GABRIEL. Aye well but it's all strategies and strategies change,
that's the point of strategies.

KATE. They're the excuses of the coward.

GABRIEL. You're not seeing the big picture. We're up against a
whole empire.

KATE. Am I not wise?

GABRIEL. Are any of us? God bless now.

KATE. You will come back?

GABRIEL *kisses her and goes.* BOYD *comes running on crying.*

BOYD. Mammy.

KATE. What is it, son?

BOYD. I had a bad dream.

KATE. Come here now to mammy and I'll sing to you and scare all the bad dreams away.

He curls up on the floor by her with his head in her lap as she sits and sings stroking his hair. Transition of light and music. Brightens to day. VICTOR comes on in his working clothes.

VICTOR. I don't know about taking the boy on this trip with me. It'll be a long day for him.

KATE. He's old enough. He'll be very disappointed, won't you, son?

BOYD. Daddy, I'll go and get my gun.

VICTOR. Aye, all right son, I'm talking to your mother.

BOYD *runs off to fetch his gun belt.*

It'll be a long day for him.

KATE. He never gets out. They have children he can play with while you're loading the cart. You can come back by the bog road. It'll be like daylight with the moon out.

VICTOR. I suppose it will.

BOYD *runs back with the gun belt but without the toy gun.*

BOYD. I've got it, Daddy.

VICTOR. I'll play with you in a minute.

She gets VICTOR's overcoat and holds it for him to put on.

KATE. I've made a lunch for you. They're your cousins. The boy should get to know your family.

VICTOR. I suppose you'r right.

BOYD. I'll get my new gun.

VICTOR. Aye, get your coat as well. Mind you, I could borrow a lorry. It would take half the time and get us back in daylight.

KATE. It would take half the fun out of it for him as well.

BOYD *has gone to the hiding place ignored by them. Takes out the real gun and puts it in the holster. Swaggers and postures and takes position to challenge his dad to a quick draw.*

Do you not remember what it was like to be out at night when you were his age? I always loved it, all the stars and the strange noises that had you scared except you knew you were safe with your mammy and daddy.

VICTOR. I'll take him in the cart and come back by the bog road.

BOYD. Daddy, Daddy, I've got a real gun now of my own. Draw,

Daddy, draw . . .

VICTOR turns. Freezes. Then KATE.

I'll beat you . . . draw . . .

The gun comes out and swings up in his hand. A frozen moment.

KATE. Paddywhack. Don't. Give me that this minute. (*Grabs it.*) You shouldn't be playing with that.

BOYD. But I found it . . . I saw you . . .

She cuffs him.

KATE. Not a word out of you.

VICTOR. Give me that.

Takes gun. Sits. Breaks it open. Bullets spill out.

Son, you could have killed me. What did I tell you about pointing a gun.

KATE. Go on you, away to your room.

BOYD. But Ma, I want to go on the cart, you promised . . .

VICTOR. Do what you mother says. Go on.

BOYD *runs out.* VICTOR *gets up and faces her.*

VICTOR. So. I don't think I have to ask what use was made of this. So you were part of it.

KATE. I wasn't. I didn't know anything was going to happen.

VICTOR. Do you expect me to believe that?

KATE. Yes. It is the truth.

VICTOR. When I'm standing with this in my hand and one bullet missing?

KATE. I wanted no harm to come to John.

VICTOR. You hid this afterwards.

KATE. You have to believe I wanted no harm to come to John.

VICTOR. He believed you and look what happened to him.

KATE. I loved him.

VICTOR. So you helped to kill him.

KATE. I did not.

VICTOR. Then who did? Who did kill him?

KATE. I don't know.

VICTOR. And you demand that I trust you while I have to earn your trust. How is it I want so much to earn your trust? I believe you, I believe what you tell me. So tell me this and then I'll trust you. Who killed him? (*No answer.*) Tell me. (*No answer.*) Who gave you this gun?

KATE. A man.

VICTOR. What man? Tell me who and I will believe you had no part in it. I'll believe that you meant no harm to my brother. I will believe that you loved him as you will never love me. I will trust you with my life . . . if you give his killer to me.

KATE. I can't.

VICTOR (*a sigh*). Aye.

KATE. I can't. It was dark. Victor, please . . . I heard the shots, I ran out. It was pitch black. Victor, you remember how dark it was that night. A man ran at me, he pushed the gun into my hands, he said, here, keep that, and he ran.

VICTOR. So he spoke. You would know his voice.

KATE. He was gasping, whispering. It could have been anybody. I couldn't see his face at all.

VICTOR. But you kept this gun.

KATE. No, Victor, I hid the gun. I hid it away so that it would be out of sight and could not be used again.

VICTOR. Why didn't you tell me about it?

KATE. Would you have believed me if I had told you I knew nothing of it? When I stood there with John's body stretched out still warm and the very weapon that had drained his life still burning in my hand? You would have killed me. That is why I did not tell you. I don't know how the boy found it. It's you encouraging him to play with guns.

VICTOR. And you really do not know who that man was who gave you this?

KATE. I couldn't see anything in the dark.

VICTOR. Aye.

KATE. It is up to you, Victor. You can believe me and trust me or you will live the rest of your life in fear of me.

VICTOR. Or I can kill you.

He lifts the gun. Then he weighs it in his hand.

The damn thing was too heavy for him anyway. He'd never have managed to get off a shot. Away in and see him, don't leave him crying.

She starts to go.

VICTOR. Am I wise to believe you?

KATE. That is up to you.

VICTOR. I owe it to my brother to look after you.

KATE. I understand.

VICTOR. Do you understand what he would expect of you?

KATE. I don't need you to tell me.

VICTOR. Aye. Well, we're equals now. Maybe we both helped to kill him. Away and see to the boy.

KATE. What will I tell him?

VICTOR. Tell him he's our son.

She goes off. WILLIE and MICK come on. WILLIE puts on the gramophone. A Dance tune. MICK serves up two dinners on the table. WILLIE helps. VICTOR sits and begins to eat. Slow and methodical. KATE comes back and sits and eats. WILLIE and MICK stand back and watch them. Stay with this silent scene as long as possible.

PLAY TWO: THE SON

ACT ONE

The same basic setting.

BOYD *stands centre stage in white shirt, black tie and black trousers.*

VICTOR *is carefully unwrapping and revealing an orange sash which he will ceremoniously put on the boy.*

MICK *and* WILLIE *come on with boxes which contain bowler hats, orange regalia, white gloves and so on, which they will hand to them as needed so that father and son end up identically dressed.*

MICK *and* WILLIE *also unroll a strip of red carpet and place a small platform on it.*

WILLIE. Look at them. I'm not even born yet and already I've got the shivers.

MICK. Will you get on with this.

WILLIE. I've seen enough. I don't want to be born.

MICK. You've got no choice.

WILLIE. Maybe your good Catholic parents hadn't but mine had. Except my Da probably said – Don't you worry, I'll pull out in time. I don't know why women fall for that one. What did he care? He wasn't going to be around to find out.

MICK. Give us that. (*As they unpack.*)

WILLIE. Mick.

MICK. What?

WILLIE. If we're going to be stuck in history why can't we be stuck in the good bits?

MICK. Such as?

WILLIE. Alice McFettridge. Well . . . no . . . maybe not Alice . . .

MICK. Why not?

WILLIE. You'd laugh. I'd be embarrassed.

MICK. Why?

WILLIE. Mary Madigan. I'd like to see her again. Like jelly on

springs was Mary. Suck you in and blow you out in little
bubbles.

MICK. What about Alice McFettridge?

WILLIE. I was 17. She was 16. She had me tormented. Two months
and I hadn't got my hand on it. But she was ripe as a peach.
And dying to fall. I was mad about her. And this night, this
night she said, yes, Willie, yes. It was the worst night of my life.

MICK. Why?

WILLIE. I'd bought these new jeans. Dead tight, you know. And
when she said yes she dropped her hand onto them and I went
off like the fifth of November and she lay back and laughed at
me. She never went out with me again. I thought I was going to
die of a broken heart.

MICK. You?

WILLIE. Don't laugh. My whole life could have been different if I
hadn't been wearing new jeans. She went to Australia. I could
have been with her. Instead of having these two. Isaac and
bloody Abraham. I don't know why Isaac didn't put up a
struggle.

MICK. Did you?

WILLIE. I didn't know then what I know now, and neither did you.
You were probably lying under the blankets reading some
banned dirty book and wanking into your sock.

MICK. It wasn't a dirty book. It was James Joyce.

WILLIE. Isaac must have rebelled.

MICK. He didn't.

WILLIE. That's only in the story. That's only the way the oul fellas
wrote it. To say to the sons, let this be a warning to you, God
gives the order, we interpret them, and if you don't give us
blind obedience you'll be the next burnt offering. Shite on
that.

MICK. Isaac faithfully followed his Da. He agreed with him. He was
willing to make the sacrifice.

WILLIE. Christ, that's a terrible thought.

MICK. I do admit Christ had a few doubts when his turn came,
hanging up there yelling, Father, Father, why hast thou
forsaken me? But you wouldn't have heard Isaac say that.
Anyway it worked out for both of them. God came through in
the end.

WILLIE. Mick. There is no God.

MICK. There is if they believe there is one. (*Pause.*) Anyway, sometimes you have to make sacrifices.

WILLIE. Do you believe that? Do you really believe that?

MICK. I lived it.

WILLIE. That's not what I'm asking you.

MICK. I don't know. I did it. And I don't know. Do we have to be consumed in the fire? I don't know. Can we say no? I don't know. Can we get free of it, the ropes, the altar, the knife, the father, the voices? I don't know.

WILLIE. The father can.

MICK. Can he? How?

WILLIE. He tied the knots. There is no God. Mick, it is down to us. Just us. Us and nobody else.

MICK. What about him?

OFFICER *walks on.*

VICTOR *and* BOYD *line up and he inspects them then mounts his platform.*

OFFICER. Gentlemen, the Empire is now at war. Now is the time for every man to do his duty and, if necessary, pay the ultimate sacrifice. These are dark days but with God on our side we will come through to glory and victory.

He steps down again.

Carry on the good work.

VICTOR. Oh we are, sir. I would join up tomorrow only . . .

OFFICER. You have important work to do. We need to grow food to feed the troops. There will be no conscription on this island. It is every man's choice to join us. It tells us how many are loyal.

BOYD. I want to join, sir.

VICTOR. You're too young.

BOYD. But, Da, I want to, I've got to . . .

VICTOR. Will you shut up now.

BOYD. But, Da . . .

VICTOR. Your turn will come.

BOYD. Da . . .

OFFICER. Carry on.

Moves away. VICTOR *hurries after him.*

VICTOR. Excuse me, excuse me, sir, I don't want to bother you now but we have a few wee problems here that are like special to the north.

OFFICER. What is that, supplies, materials, money, what?

VICTOR. It's them down south, sir, wanting to come up here.

OFFICER. So? Many of them have come to join the army.

VICTOR. That's because it's a job, sir. But you can't trust them.

OFFICER. They take an oath.

VICTOR. Aye, but they won't mean it. You have to watch them.

OFFICER. I have a war to fight. I'll take all the men I can get. Now, is there anything else?

VICTOR. What about the ones that don't join up but want to come up here? What about them? And why is the south neutral, sir? Can you tell me that? Why isn't it on our side?

OFFICER. It is their choice.

VICTOR. You make a big mistake if you think that. They're just waiting their opportunity.

OFFICER. I have no time for this. I am here to mobilise all the resources of the north for war effort.

VICTOR. Don't you worry, sir, we'll defend the north. We won't let them up here.

OFFICER. It is not the south we are fighting.

VICTOR. Then let them stay where they are.

OFFICER. But I need them. They're skilled. They're unemployed at home. They want to work. I need men for the shipyards, the aircraft factories, the farms. I need labour. Men. Not boys.

BOYD. I can do my bit.

VICTOR. We don't want them.

OFFICER. The needs of the war effort come first. Now, if you'll let me get on.

VICTOR. You can't have them come up here to take the jobs of the boys who have gone off to fight.

OFFICER. It is only for the duration of the emergency.

VICTOR. Do you not understand? They won't go home afterwards.

OFFICER. I have a great deal to do.

VICTOR. I'm telling you. Sir.

OFFICER. There are much greater interests at stake than your parochial ones.

VICTOR. There will be riots if you bring them up.

OFFICER. Are you threatening me?

VICTOR. No, sir, just explaining the situation. Our loyal sons volunteer to fight for you. Off they go. The south stays neutral. At the same time they've passed a law claiming the territorial right to all of this island. This island that you divided as a reward for our loyalty to your Empire. Now you want to invite them up here. They take over the jobs, get settled, get the vote. And you're telling me they'll give up those jobs when this war's over. What happens when our boys get back home? There'd be hell to pay. And I won't stand by and let you do it.

OFFICER. I will consider what you say.

VICTOR. I think you'll do more than that.

OFFICER. That sounds very like subversion.

VICTOR. No, sir, loyalty. We'll help you fight your war, you'll help us fight ours, and we'll get on grand. We have the harbours that command the sea lanes to your allies in the west. We have the factories, the shipyards, the fighting men. They're all yours. If it's still ours when the boys come home.

OFFICER. You have nothing to fear.

VICTOR. I think you do. You don't want uproar at your back. Don't forget they had their uprising bang in the middle of your last war.

OFFICER. Why the hell can't you all get on together?

VICTOR. You're the one that's going to war, sir.

OFFICER. We will bring the workers from the mainland.

VICTOR. With return tickets.

OFFICER. With limited contracts.

VICTOR. Thank you, sir, you can count on us, sir.

OFFICER. I'll tell you what you can count on. The interests of the Empire come first. They will always come first. You had better be sure your interests match with ours.

VICTOR. Whatever you say, sir.

> OFFICER *goes off.*

And he thinks I'm thick as pig shit? I tell you this, boy, never dance to another man's tune unless it suits you. We'll do well out of this war. There's money in loyalty. You'll have something to inherit. Something your mother's family would give their eye teeth for. Aye, you and your new baby brother can be riding high.

BOYD. Will it be a boy, Daddy?

VICTOR. It had better be. I want a son.

BOYD. But I'm your son.

VICTOR. Aye, so you are. And the image of my brother.

> MICK *and* WILLIE *have moved into the house and bring on bunches of flowers and put them about.*

> VICTOR *and* BOYD *walk into it. Take off regalia. Back in boxes.* MICK *and* WILLIE *shift the boxes.*

BOYD. What happened to my Uncle John?

VICTOR. He was killed by those bastards from over the border. On patrol. Never you forget it.

BOYD. Was he my Daddy first?

VICTOR. No, he was not. You were born the full time after his death. After I took over this house and took your mother with it. Who put that idea in your head?

BOYD. Nobody. What was he like?

VICTOR. He was soft. I'll go and see how your mother is.

> *He goes in the back.* BOYD *gets out bottle and glass. Sneaks a quick drink for himself. Off stage a Baby's wail.* VICTOR *comes back.* BOYD *pours him a drink.*

BOYD. What's happened?

VICTOR. It's a girl. Aye. Well.

> *Downs drink.* WILLIE *and* MICK *start to bring on heavy blackout drapes to hang over doors and windows.*

I have something for you. So you wouldn't feel left out.

> MICK *and* WILLIE *remove flowers.*

BOYD. A present? For me? What is it?

> *Goes off.* BOYD *waits excited.* VICTOR *comes back with hands behind*

his back.

Brings from behind his back a rifle.

VICTOR. Your first real gun.

BOYD. At last. That's great. It's great. Thanks, Da. (*Handling it with glee.*)

VICTOR. You mind how you use it. And all I've taught you.

He goes off. BOYD tries out the gun. Then sneaks a drink from the bottle. Fires on imaginary enemies. Mad to go to war.

MICK. I think we should get pissed.

WILLIE. I think we'll need to. ·

BOYD *marches off with the rifle.* WILLIE *grabs bottle and drinks.*

Christ, I thought I was a big man the first time I pulled a trigger. (*Passes bottle.*) Did you?

MICK. No. (*Drinks.*) I missed.

Puts bottle down, they go off. Lights and music change. ANNE, the daughter, comes on with a doll and sits on the floor playing with it. KATE comes on with work to do, sewing, knitting, whatever, and sits at the table. Warm light. Then blackout up.

ANNE. Mammy, why is it always dark?

KATE. Because we can't show a light.

ANNE. Why, mammy?

KATE. The bombers might see it.

ANNE. Why, mammy?

KATE. Then they can drop their bombs on us.

ANNE. Why, mammy?

KATE. To try to harm us.

ANNE. Why, mammy?

KATE. They want to win this war.

ANNE. Why, mammy?

KATE. Because they started it.

ANNE. Why, mammy?

KATE. So they can take our land.

ANNE. Why, mammy?

KATE. Then their leader can tell us what to do.

ANNE. Why, mammy?

KATE. Probably because he's a man.

ANNE. Why, mammy?

KATE. Because men want to do that.

ANNE. Why, mammy?

KATE. Because they want to have power.

ANNE. Why mammy?

KATE. Because they're men.

ANNE. Why, mammy?

KATE. Because God made them that way.

ANNE. Why, mammy?

KATE. Because God is a man.

ANNE. Why, mammy?

KATE. Because he has a big beard.

ANNE. Why, mammy?

KATE. Because they didn't have razors in those days.

ANNE. Why, mammy?

KATE. Because God didn't make any.

ANNE. Why, mammy?

KATE. Because Adam forgot to put them on the shopping list.

ANNE. Why, mammy?

KATE. Because he was tormented by children asking why mammy.

ANNE. Why, mammy? (*Laughs.*)

KATE. Are you trying to make a cod of your old mother?

ANNE. I won't let that man take over.

KATE. And how are you going to stop him?

ANNE. I'm going to laugh at him.

KATE. Ah darling.

Gets down and hugs her.

ANNE. Mammy, why does Daddy go out at night?

KATE. He goes out to guard the world. All I can say is God help the world. Now it's time for bed.

ANNE. Can I see the moon tonight?

KATE. You know we shouldn't open the curtains.

ANNE. Please mammy, we can put the light out.

KATE. All right.

Puts out the lamp. Opens curtain a crack. A shaft of light falls on ANNE *looking out.* KATE *watches.*

KATE. Maybe I was wrong to want a son to fight for me.

Closes the curtains and shoos her to bed. Comes back as lights change. Priest comes on. They kneel.

KATE. Father, forgive me, I have had bad thoughts.

PRIEST. Tell me.

KATE. I want to kill my husband.

PRIEST. Ah.

KATE. I wish he was dead.

PRIEST. Ah.

KATE. I wish I had this house to myself.

PRIEST. Do you?

KATE. I want it for myself and my daughter.

PRIEST. But what about your son?

KATE. He doesn't listen to me anymore. All he thinks of is the war. He can't wait to be old enough to go. I don't want him to go.

PRIEST. What does his father want?

KATE. His father is dead.

PRIEST. But you have just said you want to kill your husband.

KATE. Yes. My husband, Victor.

PRIEST. Then who is the boy's father?

KATE. Isn't that what torments me? I don't know.

PRIEST. You don't know his name?

KATE. No. I don't know which one it was. It was all at the one time. There was John and me happy and then John was dead and there was Victor.

PRIEST. John was your first husband?

KATE. Yes.

PRIEST. And who does the boy take after?

KATE. He looks like John but he has grown up to be like Victor. I so wanted him to be like John. To protect me like John. But John was killed. And I helped to kill him.

PRIEST. I'm sure you didn't.

KATE. Father, I hid the gun that was used. I know who did it and I hid their name. Doesn't that make me part of it?

PRIEST. Not necessarily. It depends . . . it depends on intention. Did you wish for it to happen?

KATE. No. I don't know. I made a curse on this divided house. I was wrong, I know I was wrong. I don't want to have these thoughts. But I don't want to live like this. Why, father, why are we divided against ourselves like this?

PRIEST. It has been done. We have to live with that.

KATE. How, father, how? When this island was divided I was left here, forced into a marriage, forced to live here in the north. In their house. Not mine. Theirs.

PRIEST. You were caught up in great events, Kate.

KATE. I was abandoned and betrayed.

PRIEST. You were given a part to play, in God's great plan.

KATE. Was I?

PRIEST. The world is at war but the Church faces a much greater battle. The battle against godlessness, against communism. And we have our part to play here. You are the lamb that is lost but the good shepherd will find you and bring you home.

KATE. How?

PRIEST. This is more than just a battle to bring about one united island, we must bring about one nation, a nation devoted and dedicated to God and his church. Where there is a prayer on every child's lips and they are safe from immoral books and filthy ideas. Where obedience, humility and chastity will be the rule. We must root out communism wherever we find it, Kate.

KATE. I'll do that. (*Ironic.*)

PRIEST. In the meantime, keep the faith. Be separate in all things. Spend your money only with your own, keep your children in our separate schools, play our own games, abstain from their houses of power for they only seek to corrupt you. Cause no trouble, but wait. Wait for the day when the power of prayer will release us.

KATE. Do I abstain from my husband?

PRIEST. That would not be right. Do only what is necessary. Will your daughter be coming to us?

KATE. Yes.

PRIEST. Good.

KATE. He doesn't mind. She's a girl.

PRIEST. But she will bear sons. Now I must be off.

KATE. So what I have to do is wait?

PRIEST. Yes.

KATE. And suffer.

PRIEST. You will be constantly in our prayers.

KATE. Just another poor bloody woman.

PRIEST. A martyr, in a great cause.

KATE. What's my penance?

PRIEST. Three hail marys. Doesn't every woman want to kill her husband sometime.

He goes off.

KATE. I think all I did was put a curse upon myself.

She goes off as lights change. ANNE *comes on and lies on the floor.* MICK *and* WILLIE *come on to watch her.*

WILLIE. Listen, what if Isaac . . . (MICK *sighs.*) No, listen, what if Isaac . . .

MICK. What about him?

WILLIE. What if Isaac was a girl?

MICK. So?

WILLIE. What do you mean, so?

MICK. What difference would it make?

WILLIE. It must make some difference.

MICK. It makes none.

WILLIE. Oh?

MICK. It's still a throat to cut, isn't it?

WILLIE. It should be different with women and children.

MICK. It's not. That's the lesson of this war. Bomb anything that fucking moves. The way to win is not fighting honourably on the field of battle but by attacking everything the armies left behind. Get yourself some fat big bombs and barbecue yourself a city with all the old and sick and young and pregnant and helpless. Torch them. Bugger military targets. Hit where it hurts. Then they'll come dancing.

BOYD comes on resplendent in a brand new airforce uniform. Mighty pleased with himself.

Would you look at him?

WILLIE. Mutton dressed as lamb?

MICK. You still tell me that story is wrong?

WILLIE. What's his mother going to say about it when she sees him?

MICK. I need another drink.

They go off.

BOYD. What do you think?

ANNE. I hate uniforms.

BOYD. Who gives a bugger what you think?

VICTOR comes on. BOYD stands to attention for him.

VICTOR. Let me see you. Grand. That's grand. Turn around. (BOYD *does.*) That's grand. Do you see that, Anne, are you not proud of him?

ANNE. I think he's stupid.

BOYD. I'll belt you.

VICTOR. Don't mind her.

KATE comes in.

KATE. What in the name of God is this?

BOYD. I joined up.

KATE. You couldn't.

BOYD. It's my birthday. Well, in a week or two.

KATE. Victor . . .

VICTOR. Doesn't he look grand?

KATE. He can't go.

VICTOR. Why not?

KATE. He's too young for a start.

BOYD. I am not.

VICTOR. Aren't you proud of him?

KATE. I am not proud of him because I am not proud of war, of killing others.

VICTOR. It has to be done. When the cause is right.

KATE. I don't want him to go.

VICTOR. He's going out to defend you and your freedom but you won't give him your blessing?

KATE. He will not have my blessing.

VICTOR. No, you will just reap the benefit of his sacrifice. I might have known we would get no thanks from you. Well, son, are you all set?

BOYD. All set.

VICTOR. Without your mother's blessing.

BOYD. Does it matter? I'm going.

KATE. He'll get killed.

BOYD. I won't.

KATE. You are sending him out to get killed.

BOYD. I'll be the one doing the killing.

VICTOR. He has to go.

KATE. Why? Why? There's no conscription here. He doesn't have to go.

VICTOR. He's old enough.

BOYD. Ma, I have to go. You can't stop me.

KATE. Why does he have to go?

VICTOR. He has to do his bit. That's what sticks with you, isn't it?

KATE. No. I don't want to lose my son.

BOYD. I'm going. I'm going to get my stuff ready.

VICTOR. Away you both go.

    BOYD *and* ANNE *go off.*

KATE. Do my feelings count for nothing?

VICTOR. Not if your loyalties don't. Can you not be proud of him?

KATE. You're sacrificing him.

VICTOR. That's the price you pay.

KATE. Ohhh, I wish his father was here.

VICTOR. What did you say?

KATE. I didn't . . .

VICTOR. Say again what you said.

KATE. No.

VICTOR. Say it.

KATE. What good will it do?

VICTOR. So. At last. At last we have the truth of it. Do you know what? I'm glad. I'll not be tormented any more. At least I know. He's John's son.

KATE. He's not.

VICTOR. What?

KATE. I was never certain which of you could be his father, but I'm sure now.

VICTOR. Whose is he? Don't torment me.

KATE. He's yours, Victor. He couldn't be anybody else's. Don't send him out to be killed. He is not John's son.

VICTOR. That's not the reason . . .

KATE. Is it not? Is that not why you want him to go. He'll have made the ultimate sacrifice. But you won't have to give this land to him. The son who might not be yours. You can give it to your next son, the one you know will be yours alone. Isn't that what you want?

VICTOR. Are you trying to drive me mad?

KATE. You want him dead.

VICTOR. I do not.

KATE. Do you love him?

VICTOR. I do. He's my son.

KATE. Then how can you want him to go?

VICTOR. It's not what we want. It's duty.

KATE. What do you feel for me? (*No answer.*) I talk to you of love and and all you say to me is land and loyalty. Listen to yourself. We have our children. They need us. They don't need history and they don't need promises, they need their lives now. They need us to make a home for them. To put everything behind us. To live together. In the one home. In the only house we have. Together. Don't let him go.

VICTOR. If he doesn't go and fight we won't have a home. He has to do it. Just the same way your brother fought for you.

KATE. What about my brother?

VICTOR. Didn't he fight for you? Were you not proud of him? Didn't he go out and kill for you? Risk dying for you?

KATE. This has nothing to do with my brother.

VICTOR. It seems the same to me. He went out to fight for you. For your future. I respect that. He had a duty and he did it. Didn't he?

KATE. I am not responsible for my brother.

VICTOR. He never killed in your cause?

KATE. I don't know . . .

VICTOR. He never fought for your freedom?

KATE. It was never a war.

VICTOR. It was. And now your son is going out to fight for you. Just like your brother. Did he never kill in your name?

KATE. I can't speak for him.

VICTOR. I'm not asking you to answer for him. I'm asking you to answer for yourself. Did he kill for you?

KATE. I never asked him to.

VICTOR. Who did he kill? For you?

KATE. This is daft.

VICTOR. Did he not have your blessing?

KATE. I didn't want him to do what he did.

VICTOR. No. He murdered your husband, my brother John. Didn't he? I suppose if he killed me you'd stand up for him. You can't have it every way that suits you. Our son deserves no less. Stand up for him. Give him your blessing. Then we can live together.

KATE. I don't know what my brother did. I never wanted

John to die.

VICTOR. He shot John. In the dark. Down the road there. As long as you keep quiet I'll never prove it.

KATE. Victor we must bury the past and let it be or it'll destroy us.

VICTOR. Admit he killed John. Admit you put him up to it. Admit you had John killed. And you can have your son home. And we'll put the past behind us.

KATE. Have the boy, Victor. Have him. But he will be your only son.

She walks off and he follows. Light change. BOYD *comes on in his uniform. In a fury. Starts to rip off the uniform. And rip down and throw out the blackout curtains. A real frenzy of destruction.* ANNE *runs on.*

ANNE. Boyd, what are you doing?

BOYD. It's over. The fucking war is over. Before I got there. It's over. I didn't get the chance. I didn't get the fucking chance to go and fight. To do my bit. It's not fair. I never got to kill anybody. It's not fucking fair.

ANNE. You shouldn't want to kill anybody.

BOYD. I'll kill you if you don't get out of my fucking sight.

ANNE. And you shouldn't swear.

BOYD. I'll fucking do . . . aaaggghhh . . . I wanted to kill somebody.

ANNE. I think you're stupid.

She runs on. He grabs up his discarded uniform and goes as MICK *and* WILLIE *come on and begin to clear up the blackout curtains. Music.*

MICK. It looks different in the light. Doesn't it?

WILLIE. It does.

KATE *comes on singing. 40's swing number, as if singing along with radio. Has water and a scrubbing brush. Attacks cleaning the table with great energy.*

MICK. Come on, let's get this done.

WILLIE. Why the hell do we have to pick up the pieces?

MICK. Because we wrecked it.

WILLIE. We didn't.

MICK. We got the blame. Because we believed in the light.

WILLIE. Speak for yourself. I was always better in the dark.

MICK. Said Alice.

WILLIE. I knew I shouldn't have told you that. I expected better from you.

MICK. Said Alice.

WILLIE. Go on, rub it in. Don't say it. (*Pause.*) What do we do now?

MICK. Said Alice.

WILLIE. I'll batter you.

> *Chases him off.* KATE *steps back to admire her clean table.*
>
> *Light Darkens.* VICTOR *and* BOYD *in B Special uniforms come on. Take their rifles and go out.*
>
> GABRIEL *comes to the border side.*

GABRIEL. Kate, Kate, are you there?

> *She comes on.*

KATE. Who is it?

GABRIEL. It's Gabriel, your brother. Can I come in?

KATE. It's not safe.

GABRIEL. They've gone out on patrol, I saw them.

KATE. It's not wise.

GABRIEL. Only for a minute. Do you not want to talk to me?

KATE. It's not that. It's just not safe.

GABRIEL. I've come all this way.

KATE. Be quiet now, the wee girl's asleep.

GABRIEL (*Coming in*). Have you a drink?

KATE. I'll get you one.

> *He settles at the table, she lights a lamp and brings him a drink. Looks at him.*

So. What do you want here?

GABRIEL. Is that my welcome.

KATE. What do you want?

GABRIEL. I came to see you, to see were you all right.

KATE. I'm surviving.

GABRIEL. I know it's been a while. With the war on I never had the chance. I've been too busy to tell you the truth. That war was the greatest thing ever happened.

KATE. Why?

GABRIEL. Rationing. The money I have made. Knowing how to get back and forth across the border. I tell you, there was a fortune just waiting to be made. We smuggled some stuff. It was good times, but that's not the best of it.

KATE. Have your drink. You shouldn't stay too long.

GABRIEL. Do you not want to hear?

KATE. What?

GABRIEL. I'm married. And I have a wee son.

KATE. I'm pleased for you.

GABRIEL. That's what I came to tell you. He's a great wee lad, bright as a button. I'm going to buy a farm in the south. Then set up a haulage business. I've got plans. I'll maybe go into politics. Get in with the right people. There's a lot of money to be made.

KATE. Is that what politics is?

GABRIEL. You better believe it.

KATE. And what about the north?

GABRIEL. I'll do business with it.

KATE. I see.

GABRIEL. I know, the dream, the effort, the sacrifice, John being killed, I know. But that was then. We've all had to grow up.

KATE. There has to be light, Gabriel. There has to be a promise of light ahead of you. No prisoner can serve their time without knowing there's an end to it. That they will be free.

GABRIEL. The fact is, Kate, nobody wants the north and all the aggravation that would come with it. It would ruin everything we're trying to build up.

KATE. But you still claim your right to the whole island? You still maintain your promise to me.

GABRIEL. It's something for people to dream about. Something to blame for all our miseries. Something to distract the headbins. If you keep people dreaming they don't notice how much money you're making out of them.

KATE. But we have to dream. It's all that keeps us going. It can't just be this. You're stuck with it, make the best of it. It can't just be this.

GABRIEL. Kate, I don't want my son sacrificed on anybody's altar. I'll have one for the road and then I must be going.

KATE (*Pouring*). How's my mother?

GABRIEL. She's grand.

KATE. I wish she could see my wee girl.

GABRIEL. One day. If God is good and we all get rich. It's peace now, Kate, peace all over the world. Things will be better.

KATE. Aye.

GABRIEL (*finishing his drink*). Well, I'm away.

He gets up to go. In comes VICTOR, *rifle pointed.* BOYD *behind him.*

VICTOR. Sit you back down. I see you've had a drink of my whisky. Pour him another one. He's a guest in our house.

GABRIEL. That's very civil of you.

KATE *pours the drink.*

Thank you. (*Takes a gulp.*) I was only passing . . . I dropped in . . . I mean, she is my sister. I wanted to tell her the news about the family and all that, that was all. Wasn't that all?

KATE. I wanted to know how my mother was.

VICTOR. You waited until I had gone out.

GABRIEL. There was no point in making things awkward. I was wrong. I see that . . . I'm sorry. But it was only for a minute. I just happened to be passing. I'll be on my way now.

VICTOR. Finish your drink. Do you know my son?

GABRIEL. No. Hello, I'm Gabriel. He's a fine young man. A credit to his father. A credit to you . . . and his mother. I'll have to go now.

VICTOR. I was waiting. I knew you'd come sometime.

GABRIEL. Just to see my sister.

VICTOR. You used to come more often.

GABRIEL. That was way before the war.

VICTOR. Aye. Before he was born. When my brother John was still alive.

GABRIEL. We were all young then. It was different times.

VICTOR. They don't seem different to me.

GABRIEL. Listen, thanks for the drink. (*Finishes it.*) I only came to say hello. I have no other purpose.

VICTOR. That's what you tell me.

GABRIEL. I swear, that's all.

VICTOR. I don't see it as different from the last time.

KATE. Victor. He just came to say hello.

VICTOR. You know nothing about him or what he has done. You're not responsible for him. You told me so yourself and I believe you. Isn't that right? So you are no part of this. He's going to have to stand up for himself. On your feet.

GABRIEL *stands up.* BOYD *moves forward to cover him as* VICTOR *puts down his rifle and steps forward and searches him. Finds nothing.*

GABRIEL. There's peace now. The war is over. I was just saying that to Kate.

KATE. That's what he said.

VICTOR. You – say nothing. Boyd.

VICTOR *takes his rifle back and covers* GABRIEL.

Put it on the table.

BOYD *goes to the hiding place and takes out the pistol and sets it on the table. The one* GABRIEL *gave* KATE *to hide so long ago.*

Do you recognise that gun?

GABRIEL. I wouldn't know anything about a thing like that.

VICTOR. You came here once carrying it.

GABRIEL. No.

VICTOR. And used it.

GABRIEL. No.

VICTOR. Now you've come here again carrying it.

GABRIEL. No.

VICTOR. I have just searched you and I found it in your pocket. Isn't that right, Boyd?

BOYD. It is.

KATE. Victor . . .

VICTOR. You know nothing about this, remember.

GABRIEL. You can't do this to me.

VICTOR (*Anger*). You are in my house. Don't you tell me what I can and cannot do in my own house.

KATE. Victor . . .

BOYD. Ma . . . shut up! (*Like a blow in the face to her.*)

VICTOR. Don't speak to your mother like that.

BOYD. I'm sorry. Ma.

KATE. Boyd . . .

BOYD. Say nothing, Ma, whatever you say say nothing.

GABRIEL. I think there's some misunderstanding here.

VICTOR. You came here before. You came with that gun. And you used that gun.

GABRIEL. Now, wait a minute . . .

VICTOR. You used it to kill a man. You used it to kill my brother.

GABRIEL. There's no proof of that. You have no proof of that.

VICTOR. I have proof.

GABRIEL. What? What proof? What proof can you have?

VICTOR. Her. (*All look at* KATE.)

GABRIEL. You said yourself she doesn't know anything.

VICTOR. Then let her tell me again. Did this man kill your husband?

KATE. He's my brother, Victor.

VICTOR. And John was my brother. Did he kill him? You hid the gun. Did you hide it for him?

KATE. I hid the gun, I told you I hid the gun. I told why I hid it. I was afraid of you.

VICTOR. You didn't tell me who gave you the gun.

KATE. I told you it was dark. I couldn't see the man. I couldn't be sure.

VICTOR. You told me you didn't know him at all. Now you're not sure. Was it him?

KATE. I didn't know anything about it.

VICTOR. That's not what I asked you.

KATE. He is my brother.

VICTOR. He killed your precious John. He gave you to me. A murder was done. You know something about it. Kate, I am asking you to tell me the truth.

KATE. I wish that was all. You're not asking me for the truth. You've made up your mind. You're asking me what side I'm on. As if we were picking football teams. I am not on your side and I am not on his. I did what I thought best to do. I had lost a husband. I did not want to lose a brother.

VICTOR. So it was him?

KATE. I wanted no more killing.

VICTOR. You wanted him alive so he could kill me.

KATE. If I did I don't now.

BOYD. Da?

VICTOR. What?

BOYD. Can you quit talking and get on with it?

KATE. Victor, please. Gabriel came here to tell me that I could no longer look to him for help. That is the truth. Let him go. Please, Victor, let him go.

VICTOR. I know all I need now.

GABRIEL. She wasn't any part of it.

KATE. I will not give you proof.

VICTOR. I don't need it. I believe what you tell me. Just the same way people will believe me when I tell them I caught this man, after dark, come over the border, with a gun. I caught him as I was coming back from patrol. It doesn't matter who knew what in the past. I have him here. Now.

GABRIEL. I didn't come with a gun.

VICTOR. Can you prove it?

GABRIEL. She will tell you, I came to say I was married, I have a wee son of my own. I'm settled, with a business . . . she'll tell you.

VICTOR. Is she your proof? The same way she is mine?

KATE. Victor, don't punish me through him.

GABRIEL. I came in peace. It's all over. All the wars are over.

VICTOR. Do you know something? That doesn't suit me. That

doesn't suit me at all. What does suit me is that you lot are back up to your old tricks. Sneaking over the border, carrying on the old campaign to drive us out, steal our land, murder us. I'll tell you why it suits me. It keeps people from going soft. It reminds them who they are and what they fought for. It keeps them vigilant. It reminds them never to trust you people. It reminds me never to trust her.

GABRIEL. You'll start the whole border war up again.

VICTOR. That suits me fine.

GABRIEL. It's crazy.

VICTOR. You'll be the proof of it.

GABRIEL. You're wrong.

VICTOR. I'm wrong? You murdered my brother.

GABRIEL. I saw a man in a uniform. That uniform made him a representative of an illegitimate state that I had taken up arms against. I shot at a uniform in a battle.

VICTOR. It was in the bloody dark. In an ambush.

GABRIEL. I didn't know I had shot her husband. I wish I hadn't. She forgave me.

VICTOR. Forgave you? She bloody helped you.

KATE. Paddywhack, Paddywhack, son, will you talk to your father, make him see sense, make him stop this.

BOYD. What do you say, Da, will we do it now?

KATE. Do what?

BOYD. I get to kill him. It was promised to me.

KATE. NOOOOOOO!

BOYD. Can I do it now?

> KATE *moves to step in front of* GABRIEL. VICTOR *lunges for her but* GABRIEL *puts her to the side.*

GABRIEL. No, Kate, stay out of it now.

BOYD. Say the word. Let me do it.

VICTOR. Not in here. He has to be outside. You take him out. You let him start to run. Everybody will believe it. No questions will be asked. Are you ready to go?

GABRIEL. This will have a terrible consequence.

VICTOR. You should have thought of that when you pulled the

trigger. You can have a drink if you want it.

GABRIEL. I do.

VICTOR. Pour it for him.

> KATE *pours and gives* GABRIEL *the glass. In the flurry no one notices* ANNE *creep in at the back clutching her doll. Watching* GABRIEL *trying to make the drink last.*

VICTOR. Afterwards you take this gun and put it in his hand and then knock it out as if he fell with it. Make sure it's only his fingerprints on it.

KATE. Boyd. You must not do this. This is murder.

BOYD. Come on you.

GABRIEL. Can I say a prayer?

BOYD. You can do it while you're running.

GABRIEL. I can't move.

BOYD. I'm giving you a chance.

> GABRIEL *suddenly sprints for the door.* BOYD *whoops at the joy of the chase. Pauses in door with rifle raised, letting the quarry run. Goes out. A pause. A shot.* BOYD *comes back and picks up the pistol and goes out.* KATE *sees* ANNE *and runs to her and grabs her to her.*

KATE. Oh my God. See what you've done this night.

VICTOR. I've done God's work. She'll learn that. Take that child to bed.

> KATE *takes* ANNE *off.* VICTOR *slumps. The taste of victory bitter.* BOYD *comes back glowing. Pours a drink for himself.*

You're too young to be . . . no, you're not too young.

BOYD. There's been some work tonight. Here. (*Pours* VICTOR *a drink.*) You look as if you need it. Get that down you and then go and get the police. You can leave all this to me.

> VICTOR *gulps his drink and goes out.* BOYD *sits on the edge of the table and pours another drink.*

> *A terrible wailing from* KATE *off-stage. He finishes his drink. Unmoved. Her wailing dies away.*

BOYD. It's mine now. This place is mine.

ACT TWO

An evangelical hymn swells out. His reverence, a fundamentalist Protestant preacher (played by same actor as PRIEST) *stands by a kneeling* VICTOR.

HIS REV. This is a great day. A day to rejoice. Rejoice that a sinner has repented. He has opened his heart to the true faith. Open your heart, Victor, and let Jesus come in. For he is the way the truth and the light. Open your heart to him and you will be born again. Can you feel him? Can you feel the spirit? Do you accept Jesus as your Saviour?

VICTOR. I do.

HIS REV. Amen. You are now washed in the blood of the lamb.

VICTOR. I want forgiveness.

HIS REV. God forgives you. God forgives all men. You are saved.

VICTOR. Thank you.

HIS REV. Don't thank me, thank God.

The hymn ends. VICTOR *gets up.* HIS REV *shakes his hand.*

Welcome, Victor, welcome to our church. This is God's work. He has called you to my church to do his work. Hallelujah, sir, hallelujah.

VICTOR. Aye.

HIS REV. We're but a small flock but with a man of your means among us we can spread the gospel and build a great tabernacle where I can preach the word.

KATE *comes on.*

HIS REV. I'll leave you then. (*To her.*) Good day. We must do God's holy work.

He goes off.

KATE. What did that man want with you?

VICTOR. I have joined his congregation.

KATE. Victor . . .

VICTOR. What?

KATE. Oh . . . you do what you will. I can't stop you.

VICTOR. He explains it. The rightness of it.

KATE. Does he?

VICTOR. We must have forgiveness.

KATE. And you think you'll get it from that man?

VICTOR. Will I get it from you?

> *He walks off as lights change and* KATE *turns to see her mother appearing at the border side.*

> MARY *wears a vast rather cheap fur coat. A feathered hat, made up. Got a few bob and determined people will know it.*

KATE. Mother!

> MARY *makes it clear she can barely bring herself to speak to* KATE.

MARY. I want to see my granddaughter. I want to see is she all right.

KATE. Anne, come here a minute.

> ANNE *comes on. A teenager now.*

ANNE. Who's this?

MARY. She doesn't recognise me.

KATE. This is your granny.

ANNE. Oh good, are you coming in?

MARY. How could I?

ANNE. Mummy, ask her to come in.

MARY. She wouldn't have the face.

ANNE. Why not?

MARY. She wouldn't dare ask me to set foot in the place where my poor son was killed. I couldn't do it.

KATE. Mother, why are you here?

MARY. Step forward, child, and let me look at you. Are you being cared for?

ANNE. I think you should ask my mother.

MARY. She couldn't care for her own brother.

KATE. That's all in the past.

MARY. He is in my prayers every day and he should be in yours.

KATE. Yes, Mother.

MARY. Didn't I ask you, plead with you not to involve him in your dramatics. You were always the same. Never content. Always making trouble. And always others had to suffer. The grief you have caused my girl.

KATE. Me? It was you who dumped me here in the first place.

MARY. I don't know what I'm hearing. Since when had I any control over you at all. You always went your own way. You made your own bed, girl.

KATE. Mother, what are you here for?

MARY. That's the welcome a mother has from her own daughter. It only confirms my own worst fears.

KATE. What fears?

MARY. That you would never make a fit mother. You care for no one but your own fancy feelings.

KATE. Mother, Goodbye. C'mon, Anne say goodbye to your grandma.

They turn to go.

MARY. I came to see would the girl like to come with me. To live with her own family. In her proper home. Where she will be safe from these heathens. Wouldn't you like to come with me, dear, to be among your own?

ANNE. Mum?

KATE. She asked you a question, give her an answer.

ANNE. No.

KATE. No, what?

ANNE. No, thank you. I am among my own.

KATE. Now go in the house.

ANNE. Goodbye, grandma. It was nice to meet you.

She goes in.

KATE. What are you after? What gives you the brass neck to come up here and ask for my daughter? You that did nothing for your own children.

MARY. You couldn't be helped. You wouldn't be helped. I want you to see some sense for once in your life.

KATE. What?

MARY. That girl will soon be thinking about boys.

KATE. I'll tell her. I'll tell her more than you told me which as I remember it was – You've lived around farmyards all your life.

MARY. That is not what I mean. I mean they will be northern boys. Their sort. Not her own kind. If she is to marry it should be someone suitable.

KATE. Like you arranged for me?

MARY. I can see the dangers of that now.

KATE. Oh you admit it.

MARY. It is too late for you but not too late for her. Send her to me. I will send her to the nuns. She'll have a proper start in life. I can afford it if that is a burden to you.

KATE. I don't know why I ever wanted to go back with you.

MARY. Do you know you are getting very like them. It must be living with them and their dangerous ideas. That shows why the poor girl should be with her own, safe from harm.

KATE. What a choice. What a choice I have between you and that man in there.

MARY. I want your answer, Kathleen.

KATE. She will never be yours. By whatever means I can manage she will have a better life than I had or you could give her. Some new life. That is not yours and is not his. Some reborn island where our feet are not forever slipping in the reeking dung of our old fears and bitterness. And you will not strut like some old hen on a midden with your cackle and your pious squawks, your nose in the dirt and your tail up twitching for the holy rooster. Here is my answer, mother. May you get piles.

MARY. Don't say I didn't warn you. And do not mock my afflictions. They were your father's fault. Him and his birth control. You'll see sense, my girl, you'll see sense. You will not stop me caring for that child's spiritual welfare.

KATE. Goodbye mother.

MARY. You never said did you like my fur coat.

KATE. No, but I smelt it. Goodbye mother.

MICK. You have a heed for that girl. God is watching.

She goes off.

Band start intro to 'Heartbreak Hotel' as KATE *goes off*, BOYD *comes on, in dark clothes, goes into the song. Combing his hair, the full to-the-mirror routine.* ANNE *comes on, laughs at him. He stops. Goes and gets a boot polish tin and begins blacking his face.*

ANNE. God. I'm bored. What are you doing?

BOYD. It's just a wee job.

ANNE. What job?

BOYD. It needn't concern you.

ANNE. It does. I live here. Why couldn't I have been born in Paris or somewhere exciting instead of this dump. Are you going out on patrol?

BOYD. Sort of.

ANNE. Why aren't you wearing your uniform?

BOYD. None of your business.

ANNE. Tell me.

BOYD. It's a job that has to be done. There's a border campaign going on. They're sneaking over the border and attacking police stations and blowing up things then legging it back to the south. It's the old Apache raiding party trick.

ANNE. So you're going out to be John Wayne.

BOYD. I like John Wayne. What's wrong with him?

ANNE. He's a hero. With a gun.

BOYD. It's better than liking Donald O'Connor.

ANNE. I don't like him. I just like Francis the Talking Mule. Anyway the whole campaign had died down. Nothing's happening.

BOYD. I know. That's why I'm going out. They're in danger of giving up. They're useless. They're only playing at it.

ANNE. So what are you going to do?

BOYD. Keep it going.

ANNE. How? Why?

BOYD. We know where the boys are living over the border in the south so we slip across, grab one or two, bring them back, plant some stuff on them, turn them loose, have the cops standing by to arrest them. Headlines the next day. Keeps the pot boiling.

ANNE. Why do you want to do that?

BOYD. It keeps politics out of it. It keeps the people who own things in power.

ANNE. That's cynical.

BOYD. Politics, Anne, is our workers asking awkward questions about their wages, their houses, their rights, all that. But if you can shout – the Indians are coming, the Indians are coming, and show them a couple of scalps, they soon start circling the wagons and you hear no more complaints. Are you for us or against us? That becomes the only question. We can get on with making money.

ANNE. That is . . . it is disgusting.

BOYD. It's the same in the south. They got what they wanted, a one church state. Are you for it or against it? If you're not you're an outcast. Keep politics out of it.

ANNE. It should never have been divided. People should have been made to work it out.

BOYD. That didn't suit the Empire. They needed us. They didn't want a rebellious island at their backs. No way. We're the price they pay. But the dream lives on and we feed off it. I'm away. You go back to your bed. Dream of Francis the Talking Mule. I worry about you, wee sister. (*Takes out a pistol and checks it.*)

ANNE. I think I'm scared of you, big brother.

BOYD. Agh don't fret yourself. Once the boys start chasing round you you'll forget about it. It's babies you want, girl, not brains.

ANNE. I'm not staying here. I'm going to University.

He goes out. She stands, angry, helpless. Goes off. Light change.

HIS REV. *and* VICTOR *walking outside.*

HIS REV. God has spoken to me. He has shown me. He has shown me where to build a new church.

VICTOR. Where?

HIS REV. That bottom field.

VICTOR. I need that field.

HIS REV. So does God.

VICTOR. Well, I suppose, if God has the price of it.

HIS REV. God needs it, Victor.

VICTOR. I can't just give land away. I have to think of my son and his inheritance.

HIS REV. This is God's land. What greater privilege could a man have than to build a church for the glory of God and the only true religion?

VICTOR. So I'm to build the church as well?

HIS REV. God has chosen you, Victor. You opened your heart to him.

VICTOR. Aye. I didn't hear the bit about my wallet.

HIS REV. It will be a loan. You will be repaid. With interest. Remember the parable of the talents. We will sow and we will reap, Victor.

VICTOR. You have only enough congregation to fill a tin hut.

HIS REV. If you build me a church I will fill it. And it will be the first of many. I have a vision, Victor. We need a great crusade. We need to restore the people to God. We can learn even from our enemies. They put their faith first. They have their own schools, their own culture. So have we too. We must be separate in every way. They have their place. This is ours. We are the true faith and we must defend it. Amen.

VICTOR. Amen. Now, about the money . . .

HIS REV. If we have a church and draw a great crowd we won't pass the plate round we will pass buckets. And the congregation will be only too pleased to support each other by only spending their money in their own shops and businesses. They will pay whatever price is asked. And so the harvest will increase. Why go among moneylenders when church funds can be put to use? A man who owns those businesses would have his reward on earth as well as in heaven.

VICTOR. It's a powerful vision.

BOYD *comes on.*

HIS REV. Will your son agree to let us have the field?

VICTOR. He'll do what I tell him.

BOYD. Do what?

VICTOR. I'm giving him the bottom field.

BOYD. You gave it to him?

VICTOR. I did.

BOYD. And what does he give us?

VICTOR. The man needs a church. The voice of God is in that man.

BOYD. This place is mine.

VICTOR. Not yet it's not.

BOYD. I see. I see.

He stands looking at them. WILLIE *and* MICK *come on.*

WILLIE. Well, this is where I come on.

MICK. Aye.

WILLIE. I think I know how Isaac felt.

MICK *holds out his hand. They shake.*

I'll see you in a minute. There's no escape for either of us.

MICK *goes off.* WILLIE *walks up to* BOYD. *And puts his hand out.*

Howya doin'. The name's Willie.

BOYD. What do you want?

HIS REV. I brought this young man. He is a member of my congregation and has been a great servant to it and to me. I guarantee you he is a good worker. But with these hard times he can't find employment. I know you need good men.

BOYD *looks at* VICTOR.

VICTOR. Give him a start.

BOYD. You're the boss. It seems I only work here.

WILLIE. Thanks very much, sir.

He and WILLIE *go off.*

HIS REV. It's a fine thing to see a son who is obedient to his father.

VICTOR. Aye.

HIS REV. This is a great day.

VICTOR. Aye.

HIS REV. The Lord be praised.

VICTOR. Aye. I've work to do.

HIS REV. I won't keep you from it.

VICTOR *goes off.* WILLIE *comes on carrying a big shovel.*

WILLIE. Did I do all right?

HIS REV. If you work hard you will have your reward. We'll both have our reward. It's our turn, Willie. We may have started with nothing but we'll end up with all of it. I want to know everything. Everything that goes on. I want to know what that young man is thinking. I want you to keep him busy. You work on the son and leave the father to me.

WILLIE. What about the daughter?

HIS REV. The young man that marries her will be a lucky boy.

WILLIE. He will that.

HIS REV. You mind yourself. This is only the start.

He goes off.

WILLIE (*hefting shovel*). Some start. Shovelling shite.

ANNE *comes on with a book.*

Howyadoing? The name's Willie. You must be Anne. I haven't seen you at the dances. Do you not fancy it then?

ANNE. My mother says I'm to study.

WILLIE. Are you courting?

ANNE. No.

WILLIE. Do you want to come out with me?

ANNE. No.

WILLIE. Don't you fancy me?

ANNE. No.

WILLIE. I fancy you. I see you going by. On your bicycle. I says to myself, that's a pair of thighs would squeeze the juice out of you. I can see. You're restless. It won't be long. I'll be around. You won't find a better dancer than me. You'll come.

ANNE. I think I'll call you Francis.

WILLIE. Why?

ANNE. You remind me of somebody.

[Music needs to be a recognisable rock tune to advance us in time.] She goes and sits at a table with her book. Light darkens. BOYD comes on with two opened bottles of stout. Gives one to WILLIE. End of a hardworking day. BOYD strips off work shirt.

BOYD. Ma, get us my clean shirt.

KATE *comes on with fresh ironed shirt.*

KATE. Who are you taking to the dance?

BOYD. You meet them inside, Ma, that way you don't have to pay for them. That collar's not right.

KATE. It'll do you. I'm not your slave.

BOYD. Listen, one day I'll bring a wife home and then you'll be put in your place.

KATE. That'll be the day.

He grabs her and dances with her as he and WILLIE sing.

BOYD. C'mon don't mind me, Ma. You're my girl. I'd never find anybody would be up to you. C'mon, Willie.

VICTOR *comes on with his bible. She stops humming.*

VICTOR. Where are you going?

BOYD. Dancing.

VICTOR. Dancing?

BOYD. Aye, Da, haven't you heard? The whole world's dancing.

BOYD *and* WILLIE *go off.* VICTOR *sits and reads.* KATE *gets on with her work.* ANNE *sits between them at the table with her studies. An interminable quiet.* VICTOR *sighing, turning pages. The little noises that drive the nerves to snapping.* ANNE *throws down her pen.*

ANNE. I can't stand this. I can't stand this anymore.

KATE. What's up with you?

ANNE. You two. This place. Everything.

VICTOR. Tell her to wheest.

ANNE. That's it. I'm going out.

KATE. Where?

ANNE. Anywhere.

KATE. You've your studying to do.

ANNE. I'm sick of it. What good is it going to do me?

KATE. All right, go and see a friend. Give your head a rest.

ANNE. I haven't got any friends here. Not any more. That's one thing education does. It separates you. Anyway everybody else is out enjoying themselves. I'm stuck here. Studying.

VICTOR. Will you tell her to get on with her work.

ANNE *comes and stands in front of him.*

ANNE. Daddy, what are you reading?

VICTOR. The good book.

ANNE. Why?

VICTOR. To save my soul.

ANNE. To stop having to talk to anybody you mean.

VICTOR. Will you tell her to curb her tongue.

ANNE. Talk to me. Talk to me and not to her.

VICTOR. What is there to say?

ANNE. I don't know.

VICTOR. What does she want me to.say?

KATE. I don't know.

ANNE. I want . . . ohhh . . . I want you two to talk to each other not just sit there.

KATE. Talk about what?

ANNE. Anything. Communicate. Daddy, will you talk to her?

He is bewildered.

KATE. Whatever we might have said has been said long ago.

ANNE. That's rubbish.

KATE. Let things be. You're young. You'll learn it's wise.

Goes back to her study. Silence again. But VICTOR *mumbling as he reads. His hand gripping and ungripping the chair arm.* ANNE *gets up.*

ANNE. I give up. I'm going out.

She goes off.

VICTOR. What was she on about?

KATE. She's young.

VICTOR. She's like you.

KATE. She won't end up like me.

VICTOR. There's nothing wrong with the way we are.

KATE. No (*Ironic.*)

VICTOR. It's all in the past. It's peace now. It is all God's will.

KATE. Aye.

VICTOR. She needs to marry and settle down.

KATE. She'll do no such thing.

VICTOR. She should be here.

KATE. Why?

VICTOR. We're talking.

Light change. KATE *off.* VICTOR *walks forward to meet* HIS REV.

HIS REV. Is that church not a fine sight?

VICTOR. Aye.

HIS REV. The first of many. In my vision, Victor, I see all of this land belonging to God.

VICTOR. All of it?

HIS REV. To God and his true church. If anything should happen to your only son, which God help us I hope never happens, this land could end up in the hands of your wife and her family.

VICTOR. I know. But it has to go to him.

HIS REV. You could put it in trust for God. Boyd could have the use of it. Then it would be safe for the succeeding generations.

VICTOR. I worry about him.

HIS REV. We should ask God for guidance. Only the voice of God can tell us what to do about your only son. Let us pray.

They kneel in prayer.

Oh God, our dear heavenly father, we open our hearts to you . . .

MICK *walks in (Now real not a ghost). Young and eager.*

MICK. Hello . . . oh . . . excuse me . . .

HIS REV. You should never disturb a man at his prayers, boy.

MICK. I'm sorry . . . I didn't realise you were . . . ah . . . I'll go away again.

VICTOR. Who are you? What do you want here?

MICK. I think my aunt Kate lives here.

VICTOR. Your aunt?

MICK. Yes, I'm Gabriel's son. I'm Mick. Are you Victor?

VICTOR. Gabriel's son. Her brother's son.

MICK. Am I in the right place?

VICTOR. You're my nephew. From the south.

MICK. Yes. If you're my Uncle Victor.

VICTOR. I am. (*Exchanges look with* HIS REV.) I'll fetch Kate for you. (*Calls.*) Kate, Kate. I'll just see His Reverence out.

Walks to side with HIS REV.

HIS REV. This is not God's answer to our prayers, Victor.

VICTOR. I hope it's not.

HIS REV. You don't know what he's come for.

VICTOR. Aye.

KATE *comes on.* HIS REV *goes off.*

KATE. Who is this?

VICTOR. This is Gabriel's son.

One frightened look at VICTOR.

KATE. Why have you come here?

MICK. To see you.

VICTOR. Was that all?

MICK. Well, I wanted to see the place where my father died.

VICTOR. Why? What do you want here?

MICK. I wanted to come and say, sir, that I regret what happened. I don't want to excuse my father but it was different times. I thought I should come and see my auntie. She is my family. I hope we can put those different times behind us. That's all.

KATE. Oh, son . . .

VICTOR. That's a fine and decent thing to want to do, young man. I have forgiven long ago as the good book tells us to do. I am sure Kate feels the same. It is all forgiven. Isn't that so, Kate?

KATE. I'll make Mick a cup of tea.

VICTOR. I have work to do.

He goes out. She embraces MICK.

KATE . . . Oh you have his eyes.

MICK. I'm sorry, I didn't mean to upset anybody.

KATE. Oh it's not you making me cry.

MICK. It must bring back painful memories.

KATE. It does. Have you . . . have you been told what happened to him?

MICK. I think I understand it. He was young. He believed in what he was doing, believed that each generation had to take up the cause, do their bit. They talk about him like a hero but my mother would never let me think like that. She wouldn't talk about it. I'm against violence.

KATE. I'll get the tea. Or would you like a drink? I think I need one.

MICK. All right.

She pours two drinks. Both a bit shaky.

KATE. You're very brave coming here.

MICK. I want to know my family. Nobody would talk about it, you see. He was shot, wasn't he?

KATE. Yes.

MICK. He was shot outside here.

KATE. Yes.

MICK. He was on a raid.

KATE. He came over the border, yes.

MICK. Who shot him?

KATE. Don't you know?

MICK. I know he was in a skirmish with a patrol of B-specials. The way the oul ones tell it he fought them off for hours till he was surrounded. I'm sure it wasn't like that.

KATE. No, it wasn't.

MICK. Still, they were doing their job, I suppose. It must be awful to kill anyone.

KATE. How would you feel about the man that killed him?

MICK. I'd feel sorry for him. People shouldn't be in that position.

KATE. No.

MICK. Who did shoot him? You must know.

KATE. I do.

MICK. I just want to know.

KATE. It was Victor, it was my husband. It was Victor killed him. They caught him. It was outside this house. Why did you come here?

MICK. I told you.

KATE. Was that the whole reason?

MICK. I don't know. I never knew my father. I wanted to lay the past to rest, I suppose. Something like that. I don't know.

KATE. And has it?

MICK. I hope so.

KATE. So do I. So do I. I'll get you something to eat. You'll have been travelling a long time.

MICK. What was he like? My father, Gabriel.

KATE. He cared a lot about you. And me. All his family. And his country. He cared. He tried. Maybe he shouldn't have listened to half the things that were said to him. Things I said to him. Like you say, it was different times. A sandwich, I'll get you a sandwich.

ANNE *comes on.*

KATE. Anne, it's Mick your cousin Mick.

She goes out.

MICK. Hello.

ANNE. Hello. (*He's staring at her.*) What are you staring at?

MICK. I didn't expect . . .

ANNE. What didn't you expect?

MICK. I didn't expect to have a cousin that looked like you.

ANNE. What's the matter with me?

MICK. Nothing. Not one thing.

ANNE. You must have given my mother a fearful shock.

MICK. I didn't mean to. I think I upset your father more.

ANNE. Why?

MICK. Well, he shot him.

ANNE. Who told you that?

MICK. Your mother.

ANNE. Did she?

MICK. You must know what happened.

ANNE. I do.

MICK. I have no bitterness. I mean, he came raiding across the border with a gun. He fired on them.

ANNE. Is that what you believe?

MICK. It was the times. I hope they're over.

ANNE. I do too. So why did you come?

MICK. I want . . . I want to . . . oh it sounds stupid . . .

ANNE. What?

MICK. I want to try to help to heal those old divisions. It does sound stupid, doesn't it?

ANNE. No.

MICK. I mean, it's different now. It has to be different now. It's our future and not their past. Isn't it?

ANNE. Is that what you believe?

MICK. Shouldn't everybody?

ANNE. I'm glad you are here. I'm very glad you are here.

MICK. Are you?

She shakes his hand, an oddly formal gesture.

ANNE. You're welcome. Will you stay? Will you stay a night or two with us? Do you want to?

MICK. I don't mind.

ANNE. Do you like rock and roll?

MICK. Live it and breathe it.

ANNE. Where are you living?

MICK. I have moved back to the north. I want to be where my family started.

ANNE. Don't you hate it up here? It's so stifling, it's so boring.

MICK. It's the same in the south.

ANNE. There's a whole world out there. I'm not going to be stuck here. I've been going mad here. You don't know how glad I am to see you. Somebody to talk to, somebody to have a laugh with.

MICK. What, no boyfriends?

ANNE. Here? Are you mad? Go out with a boy twice here and they have you married. No fear. What about you?

MICK. No. I'm just . . .

ANNE. Slow?

MICK. Frightened, I think.

ANNE. Of what?

MICK. Girls.

ANNE. That sounds like a challenge. Will we go dancing?

MICK. We're cousins.

ANNE. Sure that adds to the fun.

MICK. But . . .

ANNE. You should see your face.

MICK. You're having me on.

ANNE. You don't know, do you? Come on.

MICK. I don't understand girls.

ANNE. You don't have to. Just enjoy it. (KATE *comes on with tray.*)
Come on. Ma, we're going dancing.

Grabs his hand and runs him off. Light darkens.

VICTOR. Where is he?

KATE. They've gone out together.

VICTOR. What did you tell him?

KATE. I told him it was you that did it. That you were on patrol.

VICTOR. I was.

KATE. Is that what you believe now?

VICTOR. No. I've prayed for forgiveness.

KATE. I know. Let it be, Victor. We can't set the young ones against
each other. You go to bed. I'll stay up and talk to Boyd.

VICTOR. Boyd can handle him.

KATE. That's what I'm afraid of.

VICTOR. Let it be. Let Boyd find out what he's after.

KATE. I wish I knew what was best to do.

VICTOR. Let it be. Enough's been done. Enough's been said.
Come in.

*He leads her in though she is reluctant. Darker. As they go WILLIE
comes on, spying.*

WILLIE (*Calling quietly, hopefully.*) Anne? Anne?

Looks round. Into house. Sits in VICTOR's chair.

Someday it will be you and me Anne sitting here. They think all
I'm good for is doing what I'm told but one day I'll be giving
the orders.

Fancies himself there. Off-stage giggling.

He gets up and hides himself. We must be aware that he is there spying.

ANNE *and* MICK *come on.*

ANNE. You're daft. And where did you learn to dance?

MICK. I didn't.

ANNE. Well that was obvious. And you know nothing about how to treat a girl.

MICK. I went to the Christian Brothers. It wasn't on the curriculum.

ANNE. Here, have a drink. (*Getting glasses and a bottle.*)

MICK. I think I've had enough excitement.

ANNE. The night's only started.

MICK. Is it?

ANNE. Everybody else is in bed. We can do whatever we want.

MICK. Don't be teasing me.

ANNE. I'm not teasing. You were just what I wanted, walking in here.

MICK. I'm not sure.

ANNE. I am. Do you know how to kiss?

MICK. I've not had a lot of practice.

ANNE. You lean across like this. (*She does.*) And gently, gently, touch. (*Lips touch.*) Then you put the girl on your knee, like this. (*She sits on him.*) And then . . . you get stuck in.

Kisses him. They get well into kissing and groping. WILLIE *is incensed. Then* BOYD *staggers in.* MICK *tries to push her off but she stays, arm round him.*

BOYD. What's going on here?

ANNE. Nothing that concerns you.

BOYD. Who's he?

ANNE. He's our cousin.

BOYD. Cousin?

ANNE. Son of Gabriel. This is Mick. He came to see Mammy. He's staying for a day or two.

BOYD *has sobered.*

BOYD. Who asked him?

ANNE. He just turned up. I asked him to stay.

BOYD. What does he want here?

Now MICK *does push her away and stands up. Holds out his hand.*

MICK. I just wanted to meet my family.

BOYD. I see you've done that. It didn't take you long.

ANNE. Take no notice of him. This is Boyd, by the way, my big
     brother.

BOYD. Shut up you. What do you want here?

ANNE. Ignore him. He's drunk.

BOYD. I'm talking to him.

ANNE. Boyd, give over.

MICK. I wanted to see where my father died.

BOYD. Why?

MICK. To . . .

BOYD. To what?

MICK. To say that was all in the past and . . .

BOYD. Get the fuck out of here.

MICK. But . . .

BOYD. Get him the fuck out of here.

ANNE. Boyd.

BOYD. I don't want you next or near this place and I don't want
     you next or near my sister.

ANNE. I don't believe this.

BOYD. Get the fuck out. Now.

MICK. I'm sorry . . .

ANNE. You stay where you are.

BOYD. You do what I tell you.

ANNE. You're drunk. (*Goes to him.*) Boyd. Think.

BOYD. I want him out.

ANNE. Let it rest.

BOYD. What do you think he's come here for?

ANNE. For what he says.

BOYD. Aye, you would believe him.

ANNE. And why shouldn't I?

BOYD. You, get out.

ANNE. He is staying. I want him to stay. He is staying the night with us, with his family.

BOYD. He'll get the fuck out or I'll do the same to him as I did to his Da.

ANNE. Boyd!

BOYD. I didn't mean that. She's right. I'm drunk. Forget what I said. It was drink talking. What the hell. Stay . . . do what you want. The whole world's dancing.

He goes out.

MICK. What did he mean?

ANNE. Don't mind him. Let's have another drink.

MICK. I didn't understand.

ANNE. And he didn't believe you.

MICK. But I am not taking up any cause. I want nothing but peace.

ANNE. Here. (*Pours.*) Drink that.

MICK. I'd rather be doing what we were doing.

ANNE. Drink it. Can you take some hard talk?

MICK. I'd like to know the truth.

ANNE. You must promise me you won't be mad and do anything that will cause harm. Promise me.

MICK. I promise.

ANNE. You have to mean it. I couldn't stand it if you didn't. Promise.

MICK. I promise.

ANNE. Kiss me. (*He does.*) I believe your lips. Boyd, my brother, killed your father. I saw him do it. I wasn't meant to. Your father came to this house to see Mammy. I don't know what they were talking about but he didn't come to attack anybody. They caught him here.

MICK. Who?

ANNE. Boyd and my father. They came back early off patrol. They brought out a gun and put it in front of him. They said it was his

and he had used it before. This was the bit I saw. Then they said
he had to run to make it look right for the police and he ran
and Boyd shot him out there and then put the gun in his hand.

MICK. It was his gun. They proved that.

ANNE. He had left it there. With my mother.

MICK. Do you know why?

ANNE. I think I do.

MICK. Why?

ANNE. I think your father killed mammy's first husband with it.
Away back. Victor was his brother. And . . . I think Boyd thinks
it was his father was killed. Now don't be mad.

MICK. I'm not. It makes sense. On this bloody island. God damn it
and its miserable history.

ANNE. Do you want to make love to me?

MICK. I . . . I want it more than anything in the world.

ANNE. Then let's you and me fuck the past away. Come on.

She leads him off. WILLIE *comes out.*

WILLIE. He won't stay long in my place.

He goes out. Bright daylight and music. ANNE *and* KATE *come on in
the house.* MICK *follows.*

ANNE. Mammy, you are oppressed.

KATE. I'm not, dear, I'm just married to your father.

ANNE (*to* MICK). You see, she won't see.

MICK. We have to explain it.

ANNE. . . . Mammy.

KATE. Anne, I do see. You shouldn't concern yourself about me.
You should look after yourselves. It's too late for me. But you're
both young, you're both educated. You have the whole world in
front of you

ANNE. But the whole point is we want to live here.

MICK. We want our children to have something better. Here.

ANNE. We want to work for that.

KATE. What is there for you here? Why can't you go somewhere
where you'll have opportunity. You have your chance. Isn't that
what we educated you for?

ANNE. You educated us to think.

KATE. I'm beginning to wonder was that a mistake.

ANNE. This is our home.

KATE. There you go again. It's not yours, daughter.

ANNE. It's yours, isn't it?

KATE. It is Victor's.

MICK. But it's yours as well.

KATE. There's no point in talking to your father.

ANNE. That's you all over. Whatever you say, say nothing. Whatever you do, do nothing.

KATE. Aye, I've learned.

ANNE. But it's because you and Daddy never talk to each other that nothing changes. You never tell him what you want. You don't ask for it.

KATE. There's a lot you don't know.

ANNE. You have rights here. You have been oppressed too long.

KATE. Will you stop saying that? I've been through all that. I want a bit of peace now. The place is his.

MICK. And we don't want to take it away from him. It's not like before.

KATE. He can do what he likes with it.

ANNE. No, that's the point, he can't. He has to learn to share it. With you. With all of us. He doesn't just own it, he's responsible for it. And that makes him responsible for everybody in it.

MICK. We just want to bring everybody together in a fair way.

ANNE. He has nothing to be afraid of. We're trying to make a new start not open an old quarrel.

KATE. How can it be done?

ANNE. You talk to him. You explain it to him. That all you want is the share which is rightfully yours. That you want your rights as a woman.

KATE. It sounds simple.

ANNE. It is simple. It's simple justice. You have the right. You shouldn't have to ask for it. But what's not given must be taken.

KATE. I couldn't do it.

ANNE. Then how will anything change?

KATE. I don't know.

ANNE. It's only Daddy. He won't deny you.

KATE. What it is to be young.

ANNE. Will you do it?

MICK. You have to be the start of it.

KATE. If I do, it will be for you, not for myself.

ANNE. Do you remember what you said to Granny? She's going to
have a new life. By whatever means I can manage she will have a
better life than you or he can offer her. Some new life, some
reborn island.

KATE. Were you listening?

ANNE. I was proud of you. I near died laughing when you wished
she'd get piles.

KATE. You . . . you were never obedient. In fact, Mick, she was a
cheeky wee brat. She'll make your life a misery if you let her.

ANNE. Let me? He's not getting the choice. I'm not even sure I'd
marry him. Well? Will you do it?

KATE. If I do . . . I'll do it my own way.

ANNE. I'll help you.

KATE. You will not. Away, away you go the pair of you. Go on.

They go off. She sits. Thinking. As VICTOR *comes in she gets up. He
sits.*

VICTOR. Where's my dinner?

KATE. Victor . . . I want to talk to you . . .

VICTOR. Can it not wait until after I'm fed?

KATE. I'll get your dinner in a minute. Will you listen to me?

VICTOR. What is it?

KATE. I've been thinking . . . I've been thinking about the young
ones.

VICTOR. When's that boy leaving?

KATE. He's not. I've been thinking about their future and their
happiness. And what we owe them. We made the kind of place
they're growing up in.

VICTOR. They should be thankful.

KATE. I think they deserve more than we had.

VICTOR. We managed.

KATE. I don't want them living in fear the way we did.

VICTOR. What is it you want?

KATE. I want us all to have a new start. With everybody having the rights they're entitled to, not just what you're prepared to give.

VICTOR. Who's been talking to you?

KATE. I'm speaking for myself.

VICTOR. It's that young fella, isn't it? That Mick. There's been nothing but trouble since he came.

KATE. He's making us face up to things we should have faced long ago.

VICTOR. He wants what his father wanted and couldn't get.

KATE. No. They're different. These young ones are different. They don't want to take anything that isn't their due.

VICTOR. She should never have taken up with him.

KATE. He's a fine boy.

VICTOR. You would think so. Will you bring me my dinner?

KATE. Not till we've talked this through.

VICTOR. I want my dinner.

KATE. Want, want. It's always what you want. What about what I want?

VICTOR. What do you want?

KATE *restrains her temper.*

KATE. The young ones deserve better and it's up to us to see they get it.

VICTOR. I thought we were talking about what you want.

KATE. I want it for them.

VICTOR. What, for God's sake, what?

KATE. I want my rightful share in this house.

VICTOR. Oh we're back to that, are we?

KATE. No. We are not going back. But we all live under the one roof, we all depend on each other. We should have the rights that go with it.

VICTOR. I've provided for you.

KATE. And I've worked for it. I have a right.

VICTOR. It goes to Boyd when I die. It's his inheritance.

KATE. That is wrong.

VICTOR. He's our son. Isn't he?

KATE. You have a daughter too.

VICTOR. Oh I see, you want your share so you can give it to that Mick fella and her with it.

KATE. No.

VICTOR. What then?

KATE. She has a right to her own share as well as me.

VICTOR. You want to divide it? Never. You won't get your hands on it.

KATE. Will you forget about that and listen for once in your life. I'm not trying to take over. I'm not saying hand it to the south. I am saying we all live here and while we do we all have rights in it and the time has come to recognise that and give these young people the right not to be forever told by you what they can and cannot do as if you were God Almighty. Those days are past and if you don't recognise that you are an even bigger bloody fool than I ever thought you were and that is saying something.

VICTOR. I have to be sure this place is secure.

KATE. But this is the only way it will be. Because we will all be agreeing to live together and put the past behind us.

VICTOR. Maybe, if everybody did and weren't just saying they did.

KATE. Does it always come back to that? Can you trust me? Can you trust Mick?

VICTOR. I wish that girl would settle down and marry one of our own.

KATE. You can't make her.

VICTOR. Well, she can't have the other fella. They're cousins. It's unnatural.

KATE. They're in love.

VICTOR. Love?

KATE. It's her choice.

VICTOR. Damn the choice.

KATE. You see, that's just what I mean. She has a right to her choice and a right to her home and we don't have the right to tell her otherwise.

VICTOR. By God I do or she'll be out.

KATE. Would you do that to Boyd?

VICTOR. That's different.

KATE. Yes. He's your son. A man. We're only women. That'll be the last thing to change.

VICTOR. Have you had your say?

KATE. It seems I have.

VICTOR. Then get me my dinner.

KATE. No.

VICTOR. I said, bring me my dinner.

KATE. Get it yourself. And wash your clothes and iron them and buy your own food and cook it and clean up your own mess. I'm doing no more. Till I get an answer from you.

VICTOR. Anne (*Shouts.*) Anne, c'mere.

ANNE *comes in.*

Bring us my dinner.

ANNE *looks at* KATE .

Did you hear me? Bring me my dinner.

ANNE. Why can't you get it yourself. Are you paralysed all of a sudden.

VICTOR. What is this?

ANNE. It's time.

VICTOR. Time for what?

KATE. Time you saw sense.

ANNE. You can roar, Daddy, but you don't frighten anybody. Things are going to be different. Get used to it.

They go out.

VICTOR. That boy is like a curse come back to haunt me. Will I never be at peace?

He sits to one side. Light. BOYD and MICK meet outside. MICK takes two cans of beer from his jacket pocket. Offers one.

MICK. Will you take a drink with me?

BOYD. I'll drink with anybody.

They sit and drink.

She's a good girl, my sister. I don't want her in trouble.

MICK. I'll be careful.

BOYD. I don't mean that. I mean this rights business.

MICK. Are you against it?

BOYD. The question is can I afford to be for it. The knife would be out for me for sure.

MICK. We need you.

BOYD. Aye.

MICK. If you help us . . .

BOYD. I shot your father. It was me.

MICK. I know. (BOYD *looks as him.*) Anne told me.

BOYD. Ah. I wanted to do it. I won't pretend to you. I wanted to prove I was my father's son.

MICK. I understand that.

BOYD. You don't. It may be that I killed the man who killed my true father, who would never have wanted me to do that. But I wanted the comfort of vengeance. Maybe I got it. Is it revenge you want?

MICK. No.

BOYD. Wouldn't your father expect it off you?

MICK. He didn't come here with a gun in his hand the last time.

BOYD. No.

MICK. So why would I come with a gun in my hand now?

BOYD. Is it behind your back? I won't blame you. I'm ready.

MICK. I'd rather have your help.

BOYD. That might amount to the same thing. My throat cut. You don't know what you've started, you and Anne. You're a pair of bloody kids with stars in your eyes.

MICK. It's a future I want, not a past. Will you help us?

BOYD *stands up.*

BOYD. Thanks for the drink. Do you know what I should have done?

MICK. What?

BOYD. I should have run away from home.

He goes off. MICK *turns back to the house. Bright light. Music.* KATE *and* ANNE *come on with plates of food. Places laid for* BOYD *and* VICTOR . VICTOR *turns away in his chair. They begin to eat.*

KATE. Do you want to eat with us? It's ready for you.

VICTOR. I'll thole.

KATE. Suit yourself.

She sits and they begin to eat. BOYD *comes on, drying his hands.*

KATE. Are you hungry, son?

BOYD. What about him?

KATE. Ask him yourself.

BOYD. Are you coming to eat?

VICTOR. Only if she sees sense.

BOYD. Are you going to go on like this?

VICTOR. I'm not going on. She's going on. And I'm not giving in to her. What kind of man would I be to let myself be blackmailed in my own house?

KATE. That's typical. If I ask you for something it's blackmail.

VICTOR. That's what it is. You may give up now for I won't.

KATE. You won't even talk about it. You won't even consider it.

VICTOR. If you give up this nonsense I might.

KATE. If I give up you won't need to.

VICTOR. You're a woman. You should be feeding your men, doing your proper job, not this.

KATE. I'm doing nothing for you till you see sense.

VICTOR. That's grand. Isn't that grand? In my own house.

KATE (*to* BOYD). Do you want your dinner?

VICTOR. Don't you be tempted by her.

BOYD. I'm hungry. I've done a day's hard work.

VICTOR. And it's her place to feed you.

KATE. I will feed him. It's ready.

VICTOR. Aye. If he gives in to you. If he agrees to hand over his

rights in this place. His own inheritance. That's some price for
a feed of spuds.

KATE. It's not that and you know it.

VICTOR. Isn't it? Isn't it? Am I not understanding something here?
It was my impression that one or two conditions laid down by
you have to be met before a man can sit down and get fed. Fed
the food he himself has worked and paid for. If he sits down
there he has to agree to those conditions first. That's my
understanding of it. Now am I right or wrong?

KATE. You're half right.

VICTOR. I'm either right or I'm not.

KATE. You only have to agree to sit down with us so that we can all
work this out together.

VICTOR. You make it sound so simple.

BOYD. It sounds reasonable to me.

VICTOR. Reasonable? Reason and your mother have never been
within a beagle's gowl of one another. If you give in now you
give in to everything. They'll have the lot off you. She's always
wanted her way in this place. She's not getting it.

KATE. There's no talking to you.

VICTOR. There's no talk needed. We are not going to divide this
place and that's that. If we divide we fall.

MICK. It doesn't mean that. Nobody means that.

VICTOR. You keep your nose out. It's nothing to do with you. It
was your bloody agitation that started all this in the first place.

BOYD. He has a right to speak.

VICTOR. Maybe. But it doesn't mean I have to listen to him. He
can't make me.

BOYD. Listen. All my mother is saying is that she is entitled.

VICTOR. To what?

BOYD. To a share in this place.

VICTOR. That's not all she's asking.

BOYD. Well you know more than I do then.

VICTOR. Answer me this. You are my only son. When I die you
inherit. All of it. Now are you prepared to give that up?

BOYD. She is my mother.

VICTOR. And if she outlives me which I am sure she will, since she's too damned contrary to leave me a minute's peace without her, I trust that you will look after her and keep her as any good son should for his mother. For her lifetime. That is not the same as giving her a share. A share that she can leave to who she damn well pleases. Now is it?

BOYD. She'll leave it to me or Anne.

VICTOR. And what about Anne's share?

BOYD. What's that?

VICTOR. She doesn't just want a share for herself. She wants a share for Anne. You see the way of it. Divide. Divide and conquer.

BOYD. It's still me and my sister.

VICTOR. Is it? Your sister will just hand it straight over to that boy there when she marries him. And then he'll be sitting pretty. He'll have his hands on her share and he'll get your mother's share. He'll have two shares to your one. Do you see now?

ANNE. I'll make my own mind up, thank you very much.

VICTOR. You intend to marry him, don't you?

ANNE. I might. And I might not. But I'll still make my own decisions. He's not going to take over my life and everything I own.

VICTOR. It's well seen you're young. It's land we're talking about. The ownership of land. And what men will do for it. What happens, what happens if he has you and one share and Boyd here has one share, and your mother is sitting in the middle deciding who she's going to leave her share to? What happens then?

ANNE. What?

VICTOR. War. That's what happens. War.

BOYD. Not if he and I don't fight.

VICTOR. Have sense. You're men. Are you all going to live together, sharing it?

BOYD. We are. We have to. It's where we live. We've no place else to go.

VICTOR (*to* KATE). You see what you've started? What if he gets two shares . . .

ANNE. He won't.

VICTOR. He bloody will. I know your mother. (*To* BOYD.) Two shares to your one. What then?

BOYD. We'll still be living in the same place.

VICTOR. He'll be top dog and not you.

BOYD. So?

VICTOR. Is he going to treat you any different when he has the upper hand than has ever been the case in this whole island north or south? Is he going to change history? Is he going to change human nature?

MICK. I can't change human nature. But I think I can do something about history. That's why I came here. I didn't come to demand you hand this place over to my side of the family. To my aunt Kate here and then me. I didn't come here to demand you hand it over to the south. I didn't come to take anything away from the people who live here. I live here.

VICTOR. On my sufferance.

MICK. The only change of ownership is that we all own it together. As what it is. The north. Then we can begin to change history.

VICTOR. Give me one reason why I should trust you?

MICK. Because I mean what I say.

VICTOR. Maybe you're not a man at all. Maybe you're where you should be, sitting among women. Maybe you would let them run your life. Your father must be spinning in his grave to hear you.

KATE. That's not fair. That's not right.

VICTOR. I had more respect for his father than I have for him. He fought for it.

MICK. I didn't come here to fight. I don't want to fight. It won't solve it. It never has. I don't want to fight Boyd.

VICTOR. Pardon me if I don't believe you. You will.

MICK. I know he killed my father.

VICTOR. Who told you that? (*To* KATE.) Did you?

BOYD. I did.

ANNE. I did.

VICTOR. Do you know your father killed my brother, her first husband, trying to get this land?

MICK. I do.

VICTOR. And you still sit there and play the saint. You're either no man at all or you're some actor.

ANNE. Daddy, this is not all about men. It is not all about Mick. It is not all about men fighting. It is about us. Your family. Your wife and your daughter. And our rights. Our entitlement.

VICTOR. Which you two will hand to him.

ANNE. No.

VICTOR. He'll get them. I may be many a thing but I'm not soft. I'll feed myself before I'll feed him.

ANNE. Will you stop making it all about Mick. It's about us. Isn't it Boyd?

BOYD. Aye well . . .

ANNE. It's about all of us Boyd sitting down here together and sharing our food. The food we made ourselves. I want all of us to sit down together. I want my share in making that food and I want that share to be mine. Married or not married, I want my own say. All of us, to have our own say.

KATE. Victor, will you listen to the young ones. If it worries you so much you can give Boyd a share of his own now. Then when you go he'll have yours and his own. Two shares for him and two shares for Mick and Anne. Make it a condition that this table can never be divided, that it is one whole. We'll all agree to that. You will, won't you, Mick?

MICK. Yes.

VICTOR. He's got no voice here. He has no share yet.

KATE. Please, Victor. Come and eat with us. You've lived all your life without trusting anybody. You have to trust sometime. You have to at least trust your own son and daughter.

VICTOR (*looking at* BOYD). I thought I could trust him.

BOYD. Maybe the question is, can I trust you?

VICTOR. What do you mean by that?

BOYD. I mean can I trust you to do the right thing by this place? I could end up with nothing.

VICTOR. Why would you think that?

BOYD. I mean the way you're going, the people you listen to. You could end up throwing all this away.

VICTOR. You have nothing to fear if you stand with me.

BOYD. You and me. Against them. And how long will we keep that up?

VICTOR. As long as it takes.

BOYD. As long as we last.

VICTOR. We've been under siege before.

BOYD. Aye, so was General Custer.

VICTOR. You can't sit down with them.

BOYD. There's no talking to you, is there?

VICTOR. There's no need. I won't surrender.

BOYD. That's not what you're bloody well being asked to do.

VICTOR. You'll see. It will be.

BOYD. Bollocks. That is bollocks, Da. Absolute bloody bollocks and you know it.

VICTOR. I know no such thing. I know you'll stand with me or you're no son of mine.

BOYD. Well maybe I'm not.

VICTOR. You are my son.

BOYD. I'm my mother's son too. I'll do what I want.

VICTOR. What do you want?

BOYD. I want my dinner. I'll decide after that what I'm paying for it. Ma, give us a bit that meat there.

KATE. Here you are, son.

He sits.

BOYD. Eat, go on, all of you, eat.

They get stuck into it. VICTOR *gets out his bible and sits and reads it, mumbling the words under his breath. Outside.* HIS REV. *and* WILLIE *come on.*

HIS REV. How is the wind blowing?

WILLIE. Against.

HIS REV. So. We'll have to tack. You know what I'm saying?

WILLIE. I do.

HIS REV. I don't have to know what course you take. Do you understand me?

WILLIE. I do.

HIS REV. You work for Boyd in there. No one must know you work with me.

WILLIE. They won't.

HIS REV. You owe them nothing. They're the owners. If it was left to them we'd all be hired hands. Doing their dirty work. Or begging at their gate. Do you know Willie where I was born?

WILLIE. No.

HIS REV. In a wee row of mill cottages. We had newspaper for a tablecloth. The cottages stood by a road. That road led to a gate, to big white gates. A Lord lived there. He sat in the parliament. Nobody ever challenged his right to rule. He was elected without ever having to show his face. But he did show his face when he came in and out of his big white gates along the road those cottages stood beside. And because of who he was when there were public works for the starving men his road was always the first to be repaired. Our doorstep used to be level with that road. But as the years mounted they put a camber on that road that his wheels rolled along so that the rain could drain from it. And where did it drain? It drained down into our door. So the result of all his efforts for the poor was that we were up to our necks in shite instead of to our ankles. But the true Lord has raised us up. This is God's land. And I swear to God we will have it. For the Lord. Are you with me?

WILLIE. I am.

HIS REV. There maybe sacrifices. But what is one life against the coming of the Kingdom of God. That is worth any sacrifice. Be about your business.

He goes off.

WILLIE. I'll mind my own business while I'm at it.

He goes off.

The meal ends. KATE *clears some things away and leaves* ANNE *to do the rest.* MICK *stands with* BOYD .

BOYD. You better not let me down.

MICK. You better not let me down.

BOYD. I've only eaten my dinner. I haven't paid the bill.

MICK. So I have to trust you?

BOYD. We have to trust each other.

ANNE. Mick, are we going out?

BOYD. You don't know what you've started, you and Anne. It's my neck.

MICK. I know it.

ANNE. Mick.

MICK. I'll talk to you in a minute.

BOYD. Are you ready to see it through?

MICK. Yes.

BOYD. You better be. I never thought I'd see the day.

MICK. What?

BOYD. That I was in danger of believing in something. Are you two coming for a drink?

MICK. No. Some friends of mine have come up. I'm going out with them. A night out with the boys, you know.

BOYD. Aye. I'll see you. Don't do anything I wouldn't do.

BOYD *goes off.*

ANNE. And where are you going?

MICK. Just out.

ANNE. Oh, who with?

MICK. Just some fellas. Friends of mine.

ANNE. Who?

MICK. You wouldn't know them.

ANNE. I can meet them. Then I'll know them.

MICK. No.

ANNE. Are you ashamed of me?

MICK. No. It's a night out with the boys. You know.

ANNE. No women.

MICK. No women.

ANNE. I see.

MICK. Look, it's no big thing. It's just some friends. They happen to be up here for the night, that's all. What are you looking so fed up about?

ANNE. I wanted . . . oh it doesn't matter.

MICK. No, come on, tell me.

ANNE. I wanted us to go out together. So that I could talk to you.

MICK. What about?

ANNE. I didn't want to talk to you here.

MICK. Why not?

ANNE. Because.

MICK. Because what?

ANNE. Because . . . oh why do you have to go?

MICK. I promised.

ANNE. Do you love me?

MICK. You know I do.

ANNE. Say it.

MICK. Listen I'll be late.

ANNE. Say it.

MICK. I love you. Satisfied. Can I go now?

ANNE. I think I'm pregnant.

MICK. What?

ANNE. I think I'm pregnant.

MICK. Oh.

ANNE. I didn't want to tell you here. But I did think you might be pleased.

MICK. It's just a shock.

ANNE. I can see.

MICK. It's . . .

ANNE. I've upset your evening, have I? I'm sorry.

MICK. No . . . it's great. It is. It's great.

ANNE. Is it?

MICK. I just need time to let it sink in.

ANNE. You've already done that bit.

MICK. What?

ANNE. Sinking it in.

MICK. I wish I wasn't going out.

ANNE. You're still going?

MICK. It's awkward.

ANNE. No. No. You go. We're independent people. I don't let you tell me what to do so I don't tell you what to do. I just thought you'd want to be with me.

MICK. We'll talk about it later.

ANNE. You'll be pissed later.

MICK. I sort of . . .

ANNE. Away you go. We'll talk about it some other time. If it's convenient.

MICK. Ah come on.

ANNE. I wish I hadn't told you.

MICK. Are you sure?

ANNE. Sure about what?

MICK. That you are pregnant.

ANNE. No, I just told you as a joke. Oh fuck off, Mick, just fuck off and get drunk. I don't need you. Anything I ever needed you for you have already done.

MICK. Anne . . .

She runs off.

Shit. That's put me in trouble.

He steps out of the house and stands undecided. WILLIE *steps out of the shadows. A toolbag in one hand, a gun in the other. He puts the gun to the back of* MICK's *neck.*

WILLIE. Stay very still. Say nothing. Just do what I tell you. You and I have a job to do. Move.

He walks him off. Light darkens. ANNE *comes out, looks around.* BOYD *comes on.*

BOYD. Hiya.

ANNE. Oh Boyd, have you seen Mick?

BOYD. He wasn't with me.

ANNE. I know.

BOYD. He said it was a night out with the boys. Some friends of his.

ANNE. Do you know who they were?

BOYD. Don't you?

ANNE. No. The pubs are long closed.

BOYD. They probably got a carry out and are drinking it somewhere. Away to bed.

ANNE. I just wanted to see him.

BOYD. He'll be no use to you in the state he'll be in.

ANNE. I wanted to talk to him.

BOYD. Have you had a row?

ANNE. Well . . .

BOYD. Either you have or you haven't.

ANNE. It's maybe worse that that.

BOYD. Has he done anything to you?

ANNE. Don't get aggravated.

BOYD. Well has he?

ANNE. It's just that I thought I knew him and now I don't think I know him at all.

There is a large explosion off-stage.

BOYD. What the hell was that?

Runs to look off. VICTOR *and* KATE *come out.*

VICTOR. What's going on?

KATE. Are you all right?

ANNE. Yes, but I don't know where Mick is.

BOYD. They've blown up our water supply. What bastard would do that?

VICTOR. I'll get your gun.

BOYD. They'll be long gone. You stay here and I'll see to it.

VICTOR. It could be an ambush. You need men with you. Where's Willie when he's wanted?

WILLIE *frog marches* MICK *on and dumps down the toolbag.*

WILLIE. I'm here. Here he is. I caught him. There's still some of the dynamite in there.

HIS REV. *appears unnoticed at the edge of the group.*

VICTOR. So I was right. You were the serpent.

PLAY THREE: THE DAUGHTER

ACT ONE

WILLIE *stands over* MICK *surrounded by* BOYD, ANNE, VICTOR *and* KATE. HIS REV. *is at the edge of the group unnoticed.* WILLIE *lifts the tool bag he brought on with* MICK.

WILLIE. Dynamite. That's what he used. There's some still in there. Look. There's your evidence. (*Shows it round.*)

MICK. I did not do this. He did. He took me at gun point to the place. He planted the explosives. It was him who detonated them.

WILLIE. Are you going to believe him or believe me? I caught him red-handed, just after he'd blown up the place.

BOYD *rushes at* MICK *and grabs him, shaking him.*

ANNE. Boyd. Don't.

BOYD. You couldn't wait, could you? You couldn't trust me. You wouldn't trust me to get you what you wanted. You had to push it. You had to show me who was going to be boss. I believed in you. I believed you were different. But you're just like all the rest. Why couldn't you have been worth believing in?

MICK. Why couldn't you have been worth trusting? He didn't do this on his own. You put him up to it.

BOYD. Don't be fucking smart.

MICK. Who else would? You set me up. You led me straight into this. I wanted to believe you. Jesus, I should have known you people can't change. You fucking betrayed me.

BOYD *flings him down.*

I didn't do this. Why would I do it?

VICTOR. Because you and your kind always have.

ANNE. Boyd, did you do this to him?

BOYD. No.

ANNE. Then listen to what Mick has to say.

BOYD. I don't have to. He was going out with the boys. Isn't that what he said to you? We all know what that means. And he wouldn't tell you who they were or where they came from or where he was going. You said yourself you thought you knew him but you didn't. That's because he's a two faced bastard. I believed you.

MICK. And I believed you. Anne, you're wasting your breath.

ANNE. Daddy, please, you can't just jump to conclusions.

VICTOR. I don't have to. I have the evidence and I have a witness.

ANNE. What are you going to do to him?

BOYD. Say the word, Da.

ANNE. No.

BOYD. He has fucking betrayed me.

KATE. Victor, Victor, please, you see where this will go. You can't do this to the young ones, not to your own. You know where this will lead.

BOYD. I'm waiting for your word.

KATE. Don't make your son kill again for you. You have to put a stop to this.

BOYD *grabs* MICK .

BOYD. Come on you.

ANNE *rushes at him.*

ANNE. Let him go.

BOYD. Willie, grab her.

WILLIE *restrains* ANNE .

KATE. Victor, this is wrong.

BOYD. Da?

And VICTOR *hesitates.* HIS REV. *steps forward.*

HIS REV. What has happened here?

WILLIE. I caught him with the dynamite.

HIS REV. I told you, Victor.

KATE. This is not your business.

HIS REV. I warned you husband. I told him this man was a subversive and all his talk of change and equal rights was a pretence and my prediction has proved correct. Now we have the evidence of the conspiracy among us. What I wonder now, madam, is how far that conspiracy reaches.

MICK. The conspiracy is between them. I did not do this.

VICTOR. Boyd.

BOYD. Say the word.

VICTOR. Lock him in the outhouse. We'll deal with him later.

BOYD. Come on.

ANNE. Mick.

WILLIE *and* BOYD *drag him off.*

VICTOR. What's your answer, Kate? Is this the same old story? You used your brother against me and you failed. Now you have his son. You tried a different way this time but when you saw it wouldn't wash did you put him up to this? Is that the way of it?

KATE. I'm thinking now that boy has done nothing.

HIS REV. He has lied and deceived all along. He has been encouraged. Are we to believe you are so gullible that you didn't know what he was about? Are you so innocent?

KATE. I don't have to answer to you.

HIS REV. Then who do you answer to? Your friends over the border? Or to your husband? It's him you should be loyal to.

KATE. Victor, don't let him speak to me like that.

VICTOR. Answer his question.

KATE. I will not. I won't answer to him.

ANNE. Daddy, we're just asking you to talk to Mick. Give him a chance to explain.

BOYD *and* WILLIE *come back.*

HIS REV. There is only one way of dealing with his like. They have to be shown that we will defend ourselves. There must be no surrender.

KATE. You can't listen to him. Mick is your flesh and blood.

VICTOR. Yours. Yours. Your brother's son. Not mine.

ANNE. And yours, Daddy?

VICTOR. How can that be?

ANNE. Because I'm pregnant. I'm going to have Mick's baby.

KATE. Oh dear God.

HIS REV. You see how far he'll go to get what he wants.

VICTOR (*to* KATE). Are you happy now?

KATE. Me?

VICTOR. Didn't you encourage this?

ANNE. It has nothing to do with my mother. Mick is my love, my choice, my life.

VICTOR. Ah, don't be stupid.

KATE. Don't say that to her. You can't turn on her. Bring that boy back. If he was wrong he will have to repent it and he will repent it. Then we will go on.

HIS REV. And we are supposed to believe him? This is all part of their same plan to take this place over.

KATE. This is my place too. God knows I worked and endured long enough in it. And you can take yourself out of my house.

VICTOR. This man is God's servant.

KATE. Then let God speak. I challenge God to show himself here. Let him show he is a God of love and mercy and forgiveness. This God of yours and his. Let him speak. What does he say, Victor? What did God say when you knelt and asked him for your forgiveness?

VICTOR. Bring the boy back. (*Silence.*) Boyd, bring him back.

BOYD *and* WILLIE *go off.*

KATE. You will not regret this, Husband.

HIS REV. You and I must pray, Victor. We must pray for guidance.

ANNE *rushes to* MICK . *As he comes back followed by* BOYD *and* WILLIE .

ANNE. It's all right, Mick, it's all right.

MICK (*pushing her off*). I'll fight my own battles.

ANNE. I told them. They know about the baby now. They know we're a family.

MICK. Is that why I'm here?

ANNE. It's all right. Just come with me.

MICK. I want to be here in my own right.

BOYD. You've got what you wanted. A bastard for a bastard.

ANNE. Mick, come away.

She leads him off to one side.

KATE. John would be proud of this day.

VICTOR. Don't speak to me of John.

KATE. I'm sorry. I'm proud of you this day.

VICTOR. I wish that gave my heart ease.

He goes off. She glares at HIS REV. *and follows.*

BOYD. So what happened?

WILLIE. I caught him.

BOYD. Why were you out there?

WILLIE. I was coming home from the pub.

BOYD. I didn't see you.

WILLIE. There's more than one pub.

HIS REV. Does that matter? What matters is the boy has been exposed for what he is. He's after you. You and your inheritance. This is only the beginning.

BOYD. Of what? What do you want here?

HIS REV. To preserve our country, our traditions and our way of life. As I am sure you do too. I am sure you will do whatever is necessary to defend it.

BOYD. I wonder is it worth it.

HIS REV. If you don't others will. You have our support.

WILLIE. I'm right behind you.

BOYD. Beside me will do fine, Willie.

He goes out.

HIS REV. That man needs watching. He might not survive this.

WILLIE. It's all different with her pregnant. I should have been the one. I'm the right one for her. I could be taking over here. That child has to be got rid of. I want my chance.

HIS REV. Trust in the Lord, Willie. He raises us up.

They go off. ANNE *and* MICK

ANNE. Mick.

MICK. What?

ANNE. Look at me. Did you do it?

MICK. So even you don't believe me.

ANNE. Just tell me.

MICK. No. The stupid thing is I was meeting some fellas who wanted to do it, said it was the only way, and I talked them out of it.

ANNE. I don't think Boyd was part of it.

MICK. It doesn't matter now. It's done. They'll all believe what they want to believe. It doesn't matter who did it. It's too late now. Why did you tell them?

ANNE. Don't you want the baby?

MICK. Yes, yes I do. But not this way.

ANNE. It's only this baby will keep us safe. Will keep you safe.

MICK. That's the point. I'm only free because of you. On sufferance.

ANNE. You are free.

MICK. It won't be about my rights, about human rights, it's back to who owns it. The only rights we'll have will be yours.

ANNE. So?

MICK. You have no rights. You're a woman.

ANNE. We'll change that.

MICK. How? What's going to make them listen? What's going to make them change? Who's going to listen to me, or you, now? Maybe it is the only way. Maybe you have to blast it out of them. If nothing is given it must be taken. Maybe it is the only way.

ANNE. Mick, Mick, listen to me. Do you love me?

MICK. Yes.

ANNE. Then we are stronger than them. We are together. Feel here (*Puts his hand on her stomach.*) We have the future here. It will be our future. They can't take it away from us. If we stay true to that they can never defeat us. Love me, Mick. That's the way to make the world explode.

They kiss and go in.

VICTOR *and* HIS REV. *come on.*

HIS REV. What if they have a son?

VICTOR. Aye.

HIS REV. Boyd has no son.

VICTOR. Aye.

HIS REV. He may never have one.

VICTOR. Aye.

HIS REV. Their boy could inherit everything.

VICTOR. They shouldn't be having that child. They're not married. They're cousins. It's unnatural.

HIS REV. Then listen to God.

VICTOR. Aye. (*Calling.*) Boyd. Boyd, come here.

BOYD *and* WILLIE *come on.*

BOYD. What is it?

VICTOR. The time has come to make this place secure.

BOYD. It is.

VICTOR. Secure for the future.

BOYD. It'll be safe with me.

VICTOR. And what if something happened to you?

BOYD. Why would it?

VICTOR. We have enemies. It has to be secure for our own. So that they will never get their hands on it. You would have the whole use of it for your lifetime. And your children should you have any. But if anything happened the land would be safe.

BOYD. Safe? Who with?

VICTOR. God.

BOYD. I see.

VICTOR. We must now place it in trust with God.

BOYD. How?

VICTOR. Through his church.

BOYD. Would that be God's church or his church?

VICTOR. His church is God's church.

BOYD. I see.

VICTOR. The future must be secure. For our own faith.

BOYD. Da, I don't know what voices you've been listening to but this place is mine. I am your only son. I will keep it safe. That's your only concern, isn't it?

VICTOR. Yes.

BOYD. So if I can keep it and keep it safe it's mine?

VICTOR. That is the way I want it to be.

HIS REV. But God . . .

VICTOR. He is my only son.

HIS REV. What about your daughter and the child?

BOYD. She'll have to get married.

WILLIE. She won't marry him. She says she won't marry anyone.

HIS REV. He'll make sure he marries her. Can't you see what he's after? He'll use any way he can to steal your inheritance. He wants it for himself and that child of his.

VICTOR. You're giving him his opportunity.

BOYD. So she has to get rid of it? We send her to a clinic across the water? Is that what we do?

VICTOR. I wish we could.

BOYD. What's stopping you.

VICTOR. I can't agree with it. I can't agree with abortion. I can't agree to terminate an innocent life.

BOYD. What do you say, Your Reverence?

HIS REV. It's not my decision. It's for the family.

BOYD. What's your advice?

HIS REV. I don't agree with it.

WILLIE. I don't either. It's not right.

BOYD. But the price of keeping this land safe is that child's life.

Nobody wants to look at him or each other.

HIS REV. When a child is born it is born to sin. It is no longer innocent.

They all retreat to the shadows round the edge. Light darkens. Off-stage the cries of a new born baby. Then KATE comes on with a cradle on a stand. Puts it down. Coos over the baby for a moment. Satisfies herself it is asleep and goes quietly out. The men gather.

HIS REV. The boy was born in sin. It is no longer innocent.

VICTOR. All the doctor will say is that it was a cot death. Are all the doors closed?

HIS REV. I must go now.

BOYD *looks at him, then lifts a pillow from the cot and throws it at him. HIS REV does not want it and passes it at once to* VICTOR. VICTOR *throws it back to* BOYD. BOYD *flings it straight back at him. This is a deadly game of who is reponsible.* VICTOR *passes the pillow back to* HIS REV *who passes it back to* BOYD.

BOYD *approaches the cot and looks down, the pillow held in both hands. He hesitates then firmly gives the pillow to* WILLIE. BOYD *stands back.*

WILLIE *approaches the cot. Suddenly presses the pillow down.* THE BABY *puts up a struggle which he hadn't expected. The tiny fight for life takes longer than any of them can bear. At the end* WILLIE *falls down beside the cot, sitting exhausted, staring eyed.*

BOYD. So we are safe for another generation.

They turn away. VICTOR *and* HIS REV. *go off opposite ways.* BOYD *lifts up* WILLIE . *But before any of them can go the rear door bursts open with flaming light behind it and framed there is* MICK *screaming a great scream of anger.*

MICK. Aaaaggghhhhhh.

He rushes in scattering everything as they cower away. The whirlwind. Rushes out. We hear ANNE *and* KATE *crying out, keening.* VICTOR *scuttles across the floor to* BOYD. *Banging starts outside.*

VICTOR. Where is he? Is he coming back?

BOYD. Stay low.

They watch the door at the back. Smoke billows. HIS REV. *grabs* WILLIE *and they crawl down front.*

HIS REV. Now. Now is your chance!

WILLIE. Chance of what?

HIS REV. To do what we must do.

WILLIE. I wish I had never heard of you.

BOYD *crawls over to* WILLIE

BOYD. Willie, Willie, come on, we have to stop him. Come on.

Then ANNE *walks on. Picks up the pillow holds it to her stomach. They watch frozen. She is quite bereft. Then a series of blows begin, solid and deliberate that strike at the foundations of the house from outside. Smoke billows. Cries and moans.*

BOYD. I'll get her out of the way. She mustn't see this.

He slowly approaches ANNE . WILLIE *lifts up a length of wood* BOYD *has his back to him as he touches* ANNE.

Anne, Anne, just come and rest, you come with me . . .

WILLIE *raises the wood at his back.* BOYD *turns. They stare at each other.*

VICTOR (*crying out*). Help. Help us. Somebody must help us. Help. Where is the army of the Alliance. They owe a debt to us. Help us.

Another bang so that the place shakes. BOYD *pulls* ANNE *down to one side.* WILLIE *steps back. Then silence. From the back in full camouflage uniform steps a* SERGEANT. *Looks around.*

SERGEANT. Oh dear. Oh dear, oh fucking dear. What a fucking mess. Fucking look at it.

OFFICER *comes in. Nods to* SERGEANT *to go out.*

OFFICER. Right. Which of you is supposed to be responsible for this place?

VICTOR *steps forward.*

VICTOR. I am, sir.

OFFICER. Well you've made a right bloody mess of it, haven't you?

VICTOR. It was him, sir, him and his friends, we couldn't control them.

As SERGEANT *and a* SOLDIER *drag in* MICK. ANNE *moves to him, they push her back.*

ANNE. Let him go, he's done nothing. It was them.

OFFICER. We are here to restore order. Then everything can be sorted out. Stand him over there.Watch him. Let everyone be calm.

SOLDIERS *take* MICK *to one side, not threatening. People gather themselves together.*

KATE. Would you like a cup of tea, seeing as you're guests here.

OFFICER. That's very civil of you. I think we all need a cup of tea.

KATE (*to* ANNE). Come on you and help me.

ANNE. No. I dare not let Mick out of my sight.

KATE. He's safe now, they can't reach him. Come on, it will do you good to be busy. They're here to help us. Come on now.

They go off.

OFFICER. Now, sir, can I have a talk with you?

VICTOR. Yes.,

OFFICER. Over here.

Leads him to one side. HIS REV. *follows.*

Now. There has been a serious disturbance here. You have lost control of the situation. You have asked for our help. Is that right?

VICTOR. Yes, sir.

OFFICER. And what help would that be?

VICTOR. They want to take over. He wants to take over. We have always been loyal to the Alliance sir, we always defended this place for you, sir.

OFFICER. Yes. So what is the problem?

HIS REV. They are not loyal.

OFFICER. And who are you?

HIS REV. I am this man's minister.

OFFICER. I see. Now. Who exactly are they?

VICTOR. That's our enemy. There.

OFFICER. Your enemy. Not mine.

HIS REV. I think you will find they are your enemy too. They want to steal this place from you.

VICTOR. We have always been loyal. You have to help us.

OFFICER. I have to follow my orders.

HIS REV. Then surely, man, you have orders to help us.

OFFICER. My orders are to restore law and good order, not to favour anyone.

VICTOR. But I own this place. You are here to help me. To do what I want done.

OFFICER. I am here to serve the interests of the Alliance. The Alliance owns this land. Not you.

HIS REV. You cannot take this man's home away from him.

OFFICER. Nobody wants to.

VICTOR. We are loyal.

HIS REV. Ask that man over there if he is loyal.

OFFICER. I don't think I need your advice, spiritual or otherwise, at the moment.

VICTOR. We were always loyal to you. We defended this place in two wars for you. Back in 1690 we suffered seige for you.

OFFICER. That was a long time ago.

VICTOR. Nothing has changed.

OFFICER. I've read the history. I want everyone to understand this. It is my responsibility to restore order. That must be accepted absolutely by everyone. This place is ours. We now occupy it. We do not want to be here. We do not want to have to sort out your problems. But since you cannot do the job yourselves we will have to do it for you.

HIS REV. Give us a free hand and we'll do it.

OFFICER. It will be done by our rules, sir. Let me put it this way. This place will be restored to you as soon as possible provided certain conditions are met. But the first priority is the establishment of order. Now. Do you accept my jurisdiction in this?

VICTOR. I'm loyal.

OFFICER. You, sir?

BOYD. Yes.

OFFICER. And you, sir.

HIS REV. So long as you do the right thing.

OFFICER. And what is that?

HIS REV. You'll soon find out what's needed.

KATE *and* ANNE *in with trays of tea.*

KATE. Here's the tea.

OFFICER. Thank you, you're very kind. Can you take it to my men?

KATE. Go on, Anne.

ANNE *is mutinous but does so.*

SERGEANT. Thanks very much, love.

ANNE. Can I give my man a cup of tea?

OFFICER. In a moment. I have to ask him a question first.

Walks over to MICK.

Clearly there has been a conflict here. It can be resolved. You live here. For the benefit of everyone. Do you accept this?

MICK. Grievous wrong has been done to me and my own.

OFFICER. Your complaints will be listened to in due course. But I am not concerned with them yet. I must first establish order. Do you accept my authority?

MICK. No. I do not accept your right to be here.

OFFICER. But you live here. You enjoy the benefits we bring.

MICK. I can do without them.

OFFICER. Oh dear. You realise this makes things very difficult.

HIS REV. You see, I told you. You see his true colours.

MICK. I want my rights here. What is not given must be taken.

OFFICER. I am sure much can and will be done for you. Provided you accept our authority.

MICK. You have no right here. You never have. You occupied this island by force of arms. You are not wanted here.

OFFICER. The majority here have voted for us.

MICK. This island belongs to all its people and no one else. It is you that has the choice here and not me. You can come to help us live together or you can come to occupy us.

OFFICER. How can I help you if you deny my authority to do so?

HIS REV. You can't trust him.

OFFICER. This is very different from sorting out a dispute. You challenge the authority of this state?

MICK. I deny it.

OFFICER. Oh dear. No cup of tea for you. Sergeant, fetch the box.

SERGEANT. Yes sir.

He goes out.

OFFICER. I'll have my cup of tea now, thank you. (*Takes it from* ANNE.)

KATE. What are you going to do?

OFFICER. Don't concern yourself. I'm sure you will see the necessity of it. I take it you support your husband in this. Don't you?

KATE. I do.

ANNE. Mother . . .

KATE. Shh.

SERGEANT comes back in with a long box big enough for a man to crawl through and open at both ends. Nods to SOLDIER who goes out and fetches two long sticks. SERGEANT sets the box in the middle.

SERGEANT (*to* MICK). Right, you, crawl in there.

He goes to block other end of box.

Right, come on, get down there and crawl. Come on.

Forces MICK on his knees and shoves him in. He and SOLDIER have poles ready.

Now. You can crawl through and we'll let you out if you just do one little thing for us. All right? I want you to sing a song. It's a very well known song, you'll have no trouble with the words. You sing it and you get out. Now we'll make it easier for you. We'll sing it too and you can join in with us. Ready?

He and SOLDIER lustily roar out 'God Save the Queen'

I don't think I can hear you. Come on, it is your national anthem. You do live here, don't you? You do collect the benefits, don't you? C'mon, laddie sing.

They bang on the box with the poles.

KATE. Stop this. You must stop this.

VICTOR. Quiet, woman.

Bang bang on box. They stop and listen.

SERGEANT. He's very quiet. Can you hear anything?

SOLDIER. Not a dicky bird, sir.

SERGEANT. Little dicky bird doesn't want to sing. Make it easy for yourself. Sing.

They bellow and listen and bang and listen.

He won't sing sir.

OFFICER. I haven't finished my tea yet.

ANNE. You cannot do this.

OFFICER. He's doing it to himself.

ANNE. Let him go.

OFFICER. Sergeant.

SERGEANT. Stand aside, miss. (*Blocks her off.*)

ANNE. Let him go.

SERGEANT. I said, stand aside. I tell you what. If you want us to let him go why don't you sing for him, that might encourage him.

ANNE. No.

SERGEANT. C'mon, sing.

BOYD. Let her alone. She's my sister.

SERGEANT. Sir?

OFFICER. Leave her be, sergeant.

SERGEANT. Yes sir.

OFFICER. Get on with it.

> *They go back to banging the box.*

SERGEANT. Come on, lad, sing.

> MICK *tries lunging out and is blocked.*

Oh no you don't. You've got to sing for your supper. C'mon you fucking little green canary, sing. He won't sing sir.

OFFICER. Give him time.

> ANNE *grabs* KATE *as the others watch this, some with evident pleasure.*

ANNE. Mother, we can't stand by.

KATE. I'll get help.

> *She rushes off on the border side.*

OFFICER. I'll have another cup of tea. We can wait.

> *They sit on the ends of the box, everyone settles into static tableau.*

> KATE *and her mother at the side.*

KATE. Mother, you have to help here. He's your grandson.

MARY. I know and amn't I demented for him. But what am I to do?

KATE. They have us by the throat. You can't stand by.

MARY. If you could just get him over to us we'll look after him.

KATE. You will have to come and get him.

MARY. Oh I don't think I could do that.

KATE. Get the men, get them here.

MARY. It would mean invading foreign territory.

KATE. But you always said it was ours. That the whole island was ours.

MARY. Well, that's only what we said not what we meant.

KATE. But that's why he's doing it. It gives him his right to do it.

MARY. He's causing a lot of trouble, that much I know.

KATE. We need help now.

MARY. But there's a whole army there.

KATE. This is your own family. You can't leave us like this.

MARY. We won't.

KATE. Then do something.

MARY. It's a question of what and how. We'll protest of course. I'll write a letter, a very strong letter.

KATE. I never could rely on you.

MARY. No, you see, we have to be doing the right thing. You see, the trouble is that boy didn't turn out like his father. He has very funny ideas, the wrong sort of ideas, ideas that challenge the authority in both our countries. We don't need those kinds of ideas stirring up the people down here.

KATE. He is being beaten to death.

MARY. Oh I don't think so.

KATE. Please.

MARY. You see, the overthrow of the north is one thing but if he wanted to overthrow the south as well with heathen ideas that's something else again. We have to be sure we don't do anything hasty that might upset the whole applecart. Now if he were to give up those rash ideas . . .

KATE. What then?

MARY. You asked me for a gun long ago.

KATE. So?

MARY. There could be plenty of guns. For the right purpose. In the right place. In the north. To free you. Not the south. We are already free. Do you understand me?

KATE. I understand you, mother. I understand you very well.

MARY. Then I'll hear from you.

She goes off. The OFFICER *drains his cup and the scene is activated again.*

OFFICER. I have finished my tea now. What is the situation, sergeant?

SERGEANT. He won't come out and he won't sing, sir.

KATE *walks in.*

KATE. Can I speak to him?

OFFICER. By all means. We would rather not pursue this. Can you persuade him?

KATE. I need to be private with him.

VICTOR. Let him be. Don't involve yourself.

KATE. He is my own flesh and blood, he is my family. And yours, no matter how you might deny it.

HIS REV. Don't trust her, officer.

KATE. Will you fuck off.

HIS REV. There you are that only proves my point.

KATE. Victor, will you listen to him or to me?

BOYD. Let her talk to him.

KATE. Will all of you step back, please?

All retire to leave maximum space. They are still present but far enough away not to hear. KATE goes to the box and gets down.

KATE. Mick, can you come out and talk to me.

He crawls out. Their heads close.

MICK. What do they want?

KATE. The same.

MICK. They want my soul.

KATE. Remember your history.

MICK. I wanted to forget it.

KATE. You can't.

MICK. It's as if there was a curse on me. Forced to follow in the same useless fight.

KATE. Not useless. It is not useless to fight for your life.

MICK. I have nothing to fight them with. Why won't my own family come and help me?

KATE. Anne. (*Calls her.*)

OFFICER nods. ANNE comes over and hunkers down with them.

You listen and then you talk to him. It is our fight and ours alone. Our aim must be to get this army out of this house. Forget everything else. We will get guns to defend it but first we

must use the old weapons of silence and cunning. Give in to
them, son. They'll set you free and then we'll have a chance.

MICK. No.

KATE. Mick, I have tried, oh God knows I tried all the ways of living
in this house and here I am. With nothing. Well if nothing is
given it must be taken. I was right in the beginning and I
should have stuck at it. You be the son I wanted.

OFFICER. You have had enough time. What's the answer?

ANNE. Do it, do whatever they want, Mick. We know it doesn't
mean anything.

KATE. But make a fight of it. Let them think you are beaten. Will
you do it?

MICK. Go on.

KATE (*to* OFFICER). He'll not do as I ask. I'm sorry.

SERGEANT. Oh dear, oh fucking dear. Stand back, ladies.

ANNE. Don't do this to him you bastard.

SERGEANT. Such language from a fair colleen. Out of the fucking
way, darling. (*They step back.*) Now, go to it, lad.

SOLDIER *beats box.* MICK *kicks from inside. Putting up the struggle.*

Now sing you ignorant fucker, sing.

He and SOLDIER *bellow out the anthem. Then box stops moving.
They stop. We hear the thin sound of* MICK *singing 'God Save the
Queen'.*

OFFICER. Excellent, excellent. Let him out, sergeant.

SERGEANT. Come on you, out, count yourself lucky. (*Hauling*
MICK *out.*) What do we do with him, sir?

OFFICER. Let him go. No, wait, just to be sure. Let's hear it one
more time.

SERGEANT. You heard him. One more time, little birdie, just for
luck. Sing.

He has to sing it all through.

OFFICER. Charming. Let him go. Now, gentlemen, we will get on
with securing the borders of this place and then we will be back.
Come along, men.

Off with SERGEANT *and* SOLDIER *who takes the box.*

KATE. C'mon, son.

She and ANNE *take* MICK *off.*

HIS REV. We can't trust that man.

BOYD. You heard him. He sang.

HIS REV. I don't mean him, I mean that officer.

VICTOR. They're on our side.

HIS REV. If it suits them. They have their own interests here.

VICTOR. I have always been loyal. They won't betray us. If we stick together. Boyd?

BOYD. What?

VICTOR. Are you with me?

BOYD. Why don't you come and have a rest. Come on.

VICTOR. I need you, son, I need you with me.

BOYD. Yes, Da. Come on.

Takes him in.

HIS REV. You had an opportunity. You didn't take it.

WILLIE. I want to know what's in it for me.

HIS REV. No matter. We have a better opportunity now. We will give them no peace. For every blow there will be a counter blow. Until we have what we want. Until this land is safe for God and his followers. You know what needs to be done.

WILLIE. What's it worth to me?

HIS REV. Would I sacrifice you? Be about your business.

He goes off. BOYD *comes back on.*

BOYD. Who's side are you on?

WILLIE. Yours. Who else's? You're the one that's going to have this place one day. If you can keep it.

BOYD. I'll keep it.

WILLIE. Mick won't stop now. He'll come after you. They'll have guns.

BOYD. We have the army.

WILLIE. Aye, you know what they'll do. They'll go charging in like a bull in a china shop and if they can't find an enemy they'll end up creating one. It's still our fight.

BOYD. We need guns.

WILLIE. I can get them. But if I'm going to protect this place I want paying for it.

BOYD. I thought you were loyal to me.

WILLIE. I think you need me, Boyd, more than I need you.

BOYD. That sounds like a threat.

WILLIE. It's war now. And there's only one way to fight fire and that's with fire.

BOYD. Maybe we've been wrong.

WILLIE. I did what you wanted. There's a price for it.

BOYD. I know.

> KATE *comes out.*

KATE. Boyd.

BOYD (*to* WILLIE). Away you go.

> WILLIE *goes off.*

KATE. Is that officer back yet?

BOYD. No, not yet.

> *A distant rumbling background of explosions.*

KATE. What are you going to do?

BOYD. Survive.

KATE. A terrible wrong has been done here.

BOYD. Ma, terrible wrongs have been done right left and bloody centre since I was born and I don't want them done to me. That's as far as I see it.

KATE. You're the only one can change that. It has to change now.

BOYD. Ma.

KATE. What?

BOYD. I love you.

KATE. I love you, son.

BOYD. I wish it was enough. I surely wish it was. Why did you leave me on my own?

KATE. When?

BOYD. After I was born.

KATE. I was ill after you. I was on my own too.

BOYD. I was left to be his.

KATE. What choice did I have?

BOYD. What choice do I have now? I don't know to this day whose I am. Who am I?

KATE. Yourself. Be yourself. Not your history. Not living up to a father living up to a father.

BOYD. It's too late.

KATE. It can't be.

BOYD. It's way too late to stop now. I have to go with him. I have to go with Victor. He's my father. The only father I have. I have to go wherever it takes me. I can't turn against him. It would be the death of him.

KATE. It could be life for everybody else.

BOYD. Do you want me to kill him? Is that what you wanted all along?

KATE. I did once.

BOYD. I know.

KATE. For what?

BOYD. For land. Mother, the truth is you sacrificed me. The deed was done long ago. And I have sacrificed in my turn. I can no more escape than a ram caught in a thicket. For love of land.

He kisses her.

Isn't love the worst of all. It makes us do terrible things. Goodnight.

He walks off. She is very alone. Then lights spring up and the OFFICER *comes on.*

OFFICER. Ah, the person I wanted to talk to. Will you sit down?

They sit at the table.

I have been making enquiries about this situation. There appears to be a question of rights here. Your side of the family have not enjoyed the full benefit of the civil values that prevail in the rest of the Alliance. I have much to offer you. Security in your home. Employment opportunities for your children. Rights and votes in councils that affect your situation. A share of power perhaps in the fullness of time. Provided . . .

KATE. Provided what?

OFFICER. Provided there is stability and loyalty to the state.

There is a huge explosion off. HIS REV. *bursts in followed by* WILLIE.

HIS REV. Have you seen the devastation that has been caused here? We demand action. We must have security in our homes. Never mind talking of changes. There can be no changes until order is restored. That was your first priority and it still is. Are you going to sit here talking while this mayhem goes on? You know who is doing this. Lock them up. We do not want to take the law into our own hands, we want to abide by the law, but they won't. So what are you to do?

OFFICER. There have been wrongs here.

Another explosion.

HIS REV. They are being done at this very minute. Do your job, man.

SERGEANT *comes on.*

SERGEANT. Sir, we've rounded up everyone we can.

OFFICER. Who's their leader!

SOLDIER *brings on* MICK .

HIS REV. Arrest that man. I demand you arrest that man.

OFFICER. I have no proof.

HIS REV. Internment needs no proof. Just take my word for it. You know this man's history. You know and I know fine what he has done. He is a subversive. A threat to the security of the state. You will have no order till you lock him up.

OFFICER (*to* MICK). Do you want to sing for me again?

MICK. Take your poisoned dwarfs and go home, Captain.

OFFICER. Sergeant, lock him up.

KATE. You can't.

OFFICER. I can and I will. We need some breathing space.

MICK *is rushed out.*

HIS REV. Well done, sir.

A series of explosions shake them.

OFFICER. So locking them up was the solution, was it?

HIS REV. We'll find his friends. You can lock them all up.

HIS REV. *and* WILLIE *go out.*

KATE. Sir, you talked to me of rights.

OFFICER. Yes, but not now. I have to get his sorted out first. Order first, we must have order. Sergeant?

SERGEANT comes on as KATE goes off.

SERGEANT. Yes sir.

OFFICER. Is he secured?

SERGEANT. Yes sir.

OFFICER. Get the men to build a cage for him. A special cage where he can be seen by everyone. We need an example here.

SERGEANT. Yes sir.

OFFICER. This is a bloody mess, isn't it?

SERGEANT. Yes sir.

OFFICER. All we can do is hit them and hit them hard, try to make them see sense and get out of here. So hit the bastards, sergeant.

SERGEANT. Yes, sir, which bastards, sir?

OFFICER. The enemy.

SERGEANT. Yes sir, which enemy, sir?

OFFICER. Our enemy.

SERGEANT. Which one is that, sir? They're all at it.

OFFICER. We have to protect the property. So we protect the owners of the property.

SERGEANT. Yes, sir.

OFFICER. One thing at a time. Let's subdue the bastards first. Our masters want to hold this place for what reason I don't fathom, so let us do our job and then we can go home.

SERGEANT. Yes sir.

Another explosion.

OFFICER. Build that cage.

They go out. Light change. KATE and ANNE on.

ANNE. He is put up there like a monkey on display. Clinging to the bars. Food shoved to him. I can't stand it.

KATE. It is their mistake. Their mistake and our advantage.

ANNE. It is my man in there. I want him out. We can't win this way.

KATE. It's rocking at the foundations. It's rotten, you know it is, it must fall. Your father will have to see sense.

ANNE. It will only make him worse. You know that. Mick and I didn't begin like this. We wanted everyone to go forward together. Not this bitter old battle. I can't stand it. It betrays everything we tried to do.

KATE. That old battle has to be resolved first.

ANNE. With gelignite and car bombs? I'm going to talk to that officer.

KATE. It will do no good.

ANNE. You see. Everybody knows before they start what the answer will be. Nobody ever tries to find out so nothing changes. God I hate this place.

KATE. You can't leave.

ANNE. I can't leave Mick. That's all I know.

KATE. You can't leave me.

ANNE. Mother, I don't want your history. I want my own.

KATE. I'll take him a drink.

They go off. It darkens. SOLDIER *and* SERGEANT *on. Knackered.* SERGEANT *gets them two cans of beer.*

SOLDIER. Sarge, why did we have to shoot those people?

SERGEANT. They fired on us first.

SOLDIER. I didn't hear it.

SERGEANT. We've got to show them who's boss.

SOLDIER. Sarge, why the fuck are we here?

SERGEANT. That's a good question.

SOLDIER. How about a good answer.

SERGEANT. You're a soldier. Right?

SOLDIER. Yes.

SERGEANT. Your job is war, to be ready for war, right?

SOLDIER. Right.

SERGEANT. Who's your enemy? Who are you trained to fight?

SOLDIER. The East.

SERGEANT. Right. If there's another war who will be on our side?

SOLDIER. The West.

SERGEANT. Right. And we're right in the fucking middle. We need the West. We need their men and we need their supplies. How do they get here?

SOLDIER. I don't know.

SERGEANT. By ship. Across that ocean past this northern corner to our ports. So this northern corner controls the sea lanes. It did in the last war, it will in the next. What do you want behind you if you're fighting in the front line?

SOLDIER. Support.

SERGEANT. Right. So think what it would be like if the island that controls your lines of supply was in the hands of people who hate your fucking guts because of all the things you done to them. And they have memories like fucking elephants. Do you want that up your arse?

SOLDIER. No.

SERGEANT. That's why we're here. To protect your arse in the big one. We do it to them or they do it to us. We're all sacrifices in the big game.

SOLDIER. But these people have rights. They live here.

SERGEANT. None of our fucking business, boy. Follow orders.

SOLDIER. Yes, sir.

OFFICER. Right. Do you want the good news or the bad news?

SERGEANT. Might as well be the bad news, sir.

OFFICER. The bad news is we are still here. The good news is it may not be forever. The politicians have got their arses in gear and we have new orders. Bring the fellow in.

SERGEANT. Yes, sir.

Nods to SOLDIER *who goes off.*

OFFICER. Whether they will work is another matter. So I propose to take out some insurance. We want to be sure we get the result that suits us.

SERGEANT. Yes, sir.

WILLIE *is brought in by* SOLDIER *. Then he and* SERGEANT *leave.*

WILLIE. What have I done? You can't arrest me. You can't prove nothing.

OFFICER. I can put you away for as long as I want under

emergency powers.

WILLIE. It's them you want to put away, not me. You and I are on the same side.

OFFICER. Are we?

WILLIE. Well, yeh.

OFFICER. Then you would be willing to help me?

WILLIE. Ah now . . .

OFFICER. It's that or be locked away.

WILLIE. What do you want?

OFFICER. I want to know what's going on, who, when, how.

WILLIE. I can't grass on my own.

OFFICER. There are advantages to it.

WILLIE. Such as?

OFFICER. Money. Our help. You can be rid of some who stand in your way. Information is a more lethal weapon than a gun, Willie.

WILLIE. I see what you mean. Aye. I see exactly what you mean.

OFFICER. There will be some things we will want you to do. I am about to make an important announcement. It will have some consequences. I want you in a position to help me. Will you help me?

WILLIE. Do I have a choice?

WILLIE *sits with him. Lights down on them talking. Lights up on* VICTOR *and* HIS REV. *at the front.*

HIS REV. Victor, there is only one way to end this.

VICTOR. How?

HIS REV. I have prayed. I have prayed hour upon hour on my knees asking God for his guidance. He has made it clear to me. And I must make it clear to you.

VICTOR. What?

HIS REV. Do you love God?

VICTOR. I do.

HIS REV. Above all things?

VICTOR. I do.

HIS REV. Do you honour and obey him?

VICTOR. I do.

HIS REV. You must sacrifice your son.

VICTOR. What?

HIS REV. You must give the land to God. Then all these disputes will wither away because no one will have any claim to the land except God. There is no other way.

VICTOR. I remember when all you wanted was a field.

HIS REV. This is God's command, Victor, revealed to me in prayer. I am only his messenger.

VICTOR. Then God won't mind telling me himself. I want to pray.

HIS REV. I'll pray with you.

VICTOR. Alone.

HIS REV. As you will.

He goes off.

VICTOR (*crying out*). God, what am I do to?

KATE *comes out.*

KATE. Victor, are you all right?

VICTOR. What have we done you and I? What have we done?

KATE. What have you done?

VICTOR. Nothing. I've done nothing.

KATE. What do you mean to do?

VICTOR. Is he my son?

KATE. He is our son.

VICTOR. Would you hold my hand? It seems to be powerful dark and I'm afraid of it. I can't see the way to go.

She takes his hand.

KATE. You could follow me.

VICTOR. Do you know the way?

KATE. We'll find our way.

They stand looking out as light fades.

ACT TWO

OFFICER, SERGEANT *and* SOLDIER *face* VICTOR, KATE, ANNE, BOYD, HIS REV.

OFFICER. I have some proposals for you, sir. It is clear to me that you can no longer command the control of your own estate. I am therefore suspending all your rights in it until certain conditions are met.

HIS REV. You cannot do that.

OFFICER. I can and I have.

HIS REV. Then on your head lies the consequences.

OFFICER. It will not serve you well to threaten me.

HIS REV. Victor, you cannot stand here and listen to this.

BOYD. Da.

VICTOR. What?

BOYD. Listen. Before you speak.

OFFICER. That is wise advice. I said that we intended to solve this. We will return your rights and powers to govern here on this condition. It must be shared. Between you and your wife. And your respective sides. That is the only proper solution. Do you accept this?

 VICTOR *looks at* KATE .

Do you, mam?

KATE. What do we share?

OFFICER. The living to be made here, the decisions that flow from it. You will receive our generous financial assistance.

KATE. I'll wait to hear what Victor says.

OFFICER. As a sign of our good intentions all prisoners held under the emergency will be released. Sergeant.

SERGEANT. Sir.

 He goes off and brings back MICK. ANNE *runs to him.*

HIS REV. Put that man back in the cage where he belongs. We will not talk to thugs and murderers.

OFFICER. He stays.

HIS REV. Then I don't, sir. You will regret this day.

He storms off, WILLIE *following.*

All look to VICTOR .

OFFICER. Well, sir, what is your answer?

VICTOR. Let me be clear, sir, about this proposal of yours to share this land. I inherited this land from my father.

I have governed it, worked it, defended it, protected it from all assault and all pretenders to it, even though her family to the south across the border in a foreign state claim they have the right and ownership of it.

They have never been able to take this land no matter who has been set against us. They can't take it now even when the vultures are queuing on the hedges of my pastures. I have oppressed no one.

I prosecuted only the enemies of my state. When I needed help from you against their assault, help I had always been promised in return for my loyalty, that help was sent. Let me be clear. Did it restore peace and good order and rout my enemies? No, it did not. Chaos is everywhere. And from the first I have been judged and found wanting as a man doing what he sees as right in the kingdom of his own home. And now you tell me I am not fit. Not fit to govern in my own home. And most extraordinary of all I am told that the land I stand on, that land is not, as I foolishly thought it was, that land is not my own. And I have no rights in it. Except the rights you choose to grant me. Let me be clear to you on one thing. Nobody will take it from me. But it seems that I must bow to the force of your occupying soldiers. You give me a choice. I can say to you now, go you to hell out of here, you and the tatters of your empire. Or I can alter all my domestic arrangements and hand over part ownership in this unstable lease to those who have long wanted it and have no right to any of it. Now tell me this. If I do, what guarantee do I have that you will not turn round tomorrow and still judge me not fit and hand my inheritance to my enemies? I have no guarantee. I have no rights here. I think you owe me more than that.

OFFICER. As you say yourself you do have choices.

VICTOR. Some choice.

OFFICER. You would have our support.

BOYD. What do we get if we agree?

OFFICER. Our support. And subsidy. This place cannot support all its people and it never will.

KATE. Because it was an unnatural division.

OFFICER. That may be. But you have your home here. We want to help you live in it together. We have no other interest.

MICK. Then give us the ownership of it and let us decide.

OFFICER. The ownership remains ours so long as the majority here wish it.

MICK. They will always be the majority.

OFFICER. It is conditional on the proposals I have to put to you on behalf of my government. There will be guarantees. I advise you to accept it and try to live together. What is your answer, sir?

VICTOR. I must think.

He walks off. KATE , ANNE *and* MICK *huddle together.*

OFFICER (*to* BOYD). Can I offer you a drink?

BOYD. Fair enough.

They move aside while OFFICER *pours them drinks.*

ANNE. Is it what we want?

KATE. I think it's all I ever did want.

MICK. It is too late. It would betray everything we have suffered.

KATE. So what should I say?

MICK. Whatever you think is right. But they will never make me sing again. And it will not give me my son back. I never wanted to wade in blood but there is blood I want to wade in.

He walks off.

KATE. What do I do?

ANNE. I have to go with him, Ma. You must do what you think is right.

She goes off. KATE *follows.* OFFICER *and* BOYD *come forward.*

OFFICER. What do you think? Will it work?

BOYD. The Ma and Da? You don't want to pay too much attention to all that oul crap he came out with. He knows what he's done. He just likes playing the big man. He knows the real choice he has.

OFFICER. Can you make it work?

BOYD. I always knew we'd have to give up something. But I don't own it to give it up.

OFFICER. But you would.

BOYD. It depends if he makes the right choice. But I think you've scuppered that one. If he makes a will leaving it all to God's church as a religious homeland you'll tell him it's not worth the paper it's written on because it's not his to give.

OFFICER. That's right. But if he leaves it to you to work as a place for all we'll give you security on it, to you and your heirs.

BOYD. Aye, if I live long enough to father one. Would you take care of Willie?

OFFICER. It could be arranged.

BOYD. I'm tired of it. I wish we had a bit of peace. Do you ever get sick of your job?

OFFICER. I can't afford to think about it.

BOYD. I tell you I get sick of mine. My tradition. I mean, do I want to hand all that on to a son. He won't thank me for it and I wouldn't blame him.

OFFICER. You can hand something very different on if this works.

BOYD. Oh aye? It's still yours. That's what I hand on, here you are, son, this home is all your own, so long as they let you keep it, and they'll come and collect one day, nothing surer. And it won't be rent. It will most likely be your life, defending whatever interests they think so important at the time. I wanted to go to war. I wanted to be a soldier like you, to fight for your flag. I wanted to kill for you. I would have. Gladly, I was that bit too young. It ended just as I started. But I got my war. Against my neighbours. And do you know what I can't work out? Am I doing it for me? Or am I doing it for you? And do you give a fuck?

OFFICER. You are nothing but a bloody pimple on the map of Europe. What makes you claim to be so damned important in the scheme of things?

BOYD. Oh yeh, sacrifice ourselves to the greater security, eh?

They have been drinking steadily. SOLDIER *dozing.*

OFFICER. More like sacrificing ourselves to politicians. We have very weak government. They are handing our country over to the rioters, the disaffected, the strikers, the poor, the envious. People have to be made to see that, to realise it, then we can get back to strong government.

BOYD. So we're pawns in that game too?

OFFICER. I have my orders here.

BOYD. Aye, well, that's all beyond my control. But the bit I can do I will do. For my Ma. Not for you. She deserves better from us than she had. I'll away and talk to my father. Thanks for the drink.

BOYD *goes off.* WILLIE *slips on.*

WILLIE. You wanted to see me?

OFFICER. What is happening?

WILLIE. They promise to bring the place to a standstill. His Rev is as red as a turkey cock. He promises all sorts.

OFFICER. He makes a mighty noise that man, but whether for himself or you I am never sure.

WILLIE. Neither am I. But we'll have to come out on strike.

OFFICER. Of course.

WILLIE. What are you going to do about it?

OFFICER. What do you think?

WILLIE. I think you and I are playing somebody else's game here. But while I can score goals I don't think I'll be dropped. Or stopped.

OFFICER. I will follow orders.

WILLIE. Aye, I'm sure you will. In the meantime.

OFFICER. Oh yes.

OFFICER *gives* WILLIE *wad of money and he goes off.*

SERGEANT. What's the orders, sir?

OFFICER. We wait.

SERGEANT. Yes, sir.

They go off. ANNE *and* MICK *come on.*

ANNE. I think it must be Christmas.

MICK. Why?

ANNE. You being here.

Then she presses herself to him. Wild kisses and passion from both. She is trying to reach him through her body.

ANNE. I missed you.

MICK. It's safer staying away. Keeping on the move.

Holding him tighter to her as he tries to pull away.

ANNE. Hold me.

MICK. I've been writing poems for you.

ANNE. I never got them.

MICK. I never sent them. I tore them up. They were crap.

ANNE. I wouldn't have minded. (*Holding on to him.*) You could stay.
Boyd would listen. You could sit at the table with us again.

MICK. No.

ANNE. Why not?

MICK. It's still their table. It's still on sufferance. It's still only the
freedom they allow us. Still what suits their bloody interests. I've
come too far.

ANNE. I want you. I love you. I want you in me. I want you to put
life in me. I want another child. Stay with me.

MICK. Why don't you come with me.

ANNE. I want to make a life. Not sacrifice it.

MICK. I have to go.

ANNE. Will I know you when I see you again?

He kisses her. They go off wrapped together. VICTOR *and* BOYD *come
on. Meet* KATE . OFFICER *comes for their answers.*

OFFICER. Well sir?

VICTOR (*to* KATE). Is it enough for you?

KATE. Yes, Victor. It was all I asked for. And it's for the young ones.

VICTOR. Aye. It is. I am decided.

OFFICER (*to* SOLDIER). Put some music on, will you.

SOLDIER *puts music on.*

VICTOR. Now, would you care to dance?

They dance a stately waltz.

OFFICER. (*to* SOLDIER). Fetch the parcel.

SOLDIER *comes on with big parcel. At the end of the dance
OFFICER steps forward. Parcel is opened and he presents them with a
big ornate clock which is set up. All applaud. Go off and leave* KATE

and VICTOR.

VICTOR. The truth of it is, Kate, I did it for John. I had to do right by him. Now let's look at this.

She sits. He winds the clock. Then all hell breaks loose. Battering on the house, breakages, chants of 'traitors, traitors'. The two crouch together under seige. Lights flash on and off.

VICTOR. Where the hell are those soldiers?

Crawls to look out.

They're standing by and watching. Standing and mouthing – This is democracy in action and we have to protect the right to demonstrate and strike. Holy Christ. What are they doing? Don't just bloody stand there. I gave you what you wanted. Back me up for God's sake.

KATE. Victor, Victor, let's go upstairs. Daylight will come. Sense will come with it. They'll exhaust themselves.

VICTOR. What have we done, mother, what have we done?

They go off. The dark house. WILLIE, his face blackened, creeps in, gun in pocket. Petrol can in hand. Door bangs open. BOYD in it, gun in hand.

BOYD. Who's there? Show yourself. Step forward.

WILLIE *does.*

You. Christ, I might have known. Put the petrol can down. Where's your gun? Take it out. Put it on the table.

WILLIE *does.*

BOYD. Look at you. do you know what I see? I see myself as my wee sister saw me and I hear myself explaining to her why I was doing what I did. And I'm sure you would say the same. I suppose His Reverence sent you.

WILLIE. No.

BOYD. Agh, don't lie to me.

WILLIE. I'm not working for him.

BOYD. So you're taking advantage of him.

WILLIE. Maybe.

BOYD. Why burn the place?

WILLIE. Why not? It's not mine.

BOYD. Is Victor not paying enough protection?

WILLIE. He's stopped paying. He hasn't long to last.

BOYD. You should have stuck with me.

WILLIE. Aye but you have a choice. That's the difference between us. There's a bigger difference between us than there is between me and Mick. In the end this place will come to you, all you have to do is lick that officer's arse. But what happens to me if you do, and we have this new peace and order? I will be in that cage for the rest of my life for the things I have done and the danger I am. Won't I?

BOYD. No.

WILLIE. I will. You'll have to put me in it. They won't let you do otherwise. If Mick goes back in, I go too, because it has to be seen to be fair. For the rest of my life. I am the sacrificial bloody lamb here. You understand me? Why I can't go with you? It's nothing personal. But it's not up to you to decide. I will get no share of this place.

BOYD. I'll give you a share.

WILLIE. Don't pull my wire. Nothing is ever given here, it always has to be taken. That's the fucking stupid tragedy of it.

BOYD. What would His Reverence give you?

WILLIE. He'll reap what he sowed.

BOYD. So what am I do to here?

WILLIE. I wouldn't shoot me. Do that and the walls fall down. The army will let us kill each other. They'll always be there to pick up the pieces.

BOYD. There must be some way out of this for you and me.

WILLIE. I wish there was.

BOYD. So.

WILLIE. So what are you going to do? Shoot me?

BOYD. No.

WILLIE. That's wise.

BOYD. But I might hamstring you.

MICK *comes in behind him with a gun. Puts it to his head and takes* BOYD*'s gun.* WILLIE *takes the opportunity to grab up his own gun.*

So Here we are.

MICK *and* WILLIE *face each other. Stand off.*

Then MICK *makes* BOYD *kneel, takes up the can and pours petrol over him, then takes out a lighter and flicks it on.*

WILLIE. Let's put the guns down and talk.

BOYD. Burn your hopes and burn your dreams. What will you gain by sacrificing me here?

WILLIE. That's what we'll talk about.

MICK. Talk.

WILLIE. Mick you and I have more in common than we have with him. We came from nothing and we have nothing except what we have taken. You've got your side organised. I've got my side organised. We have responsibilities. We're paying out wages, pensions, funds for dependants of fellas in gaol. It all costs money. Well, we're finding the ways, the ways of making money. We're long past bank robberies, we're learning how to make money work. If we take over enough businesses we could own the place. We have interests to protect now. They divided it. Let's you and me, the people here, let's you and me divide it up. Our way. To suit us. You don't kill me, I don't kill you.

MICK. I hear what you're saying.

WILLIE. There'll still be casualties. There will be fucking dickheads on both our sides. I don't need them, you don't need them. So you do me a favour I'll do you a favour. We have some butchers among us, I'll make sure you have them. You run your scams and skims and protection rackets and I'll run mine. We all make money. What do you say?

MICK. What then?

WILLIE. Keep the pot boiling and the cash rolls in. If they build it up we blow it down and we skim the wages of every worker who rebuilds it. It's nice. We're entrepreneurs. We've invented an economy where there wasn't one. We're making money go round. So long as we don't waste too much energy fighting each other. Just don't do an Al Capone.

MICK. What?

WILLIE. Don't fiddle your income tax. Get an accountant. I have.

MICK. It doesn't solve it, Willie.

WILLIE. What the fuck? We make hay.

MICK. I want it all. I paid for it.

WILLIE. So did I. Now I'm getting something back.

MICK. I want ownership. The army has to go.

He smashes the clock.

Time stops. It stops now. Until they go.

Clock remains with glass broken and hands stopped.

WILLIE. That's the price.

MICK. You don't want them either.

WILLIE. Listen I've seen what it was like for you to be the minority, I don't want my turn on the same fun fair. Nobody 's winning here. Call it a draw and let's get what we can out of it.

MICK. That is the difference between you and me. Belief.

WILLIE. I don't see you dying for it. I see plenty of others. That's fucking hypocrisy. Let's talk sense. What do you say?

MICK. What are you going to tell Army Intelligence?

WILLIE. What are you going to tell them?

MICK. Whatever suits me.

WILLIE. Same here.

MICK. The rest we'll talk about but that clock stands.

WILLIE. What do we do with him? I was going to torch the place.

MICK. No.

WILLIE. You're right. It's too valuable. We'll torch the barn.

MICK. Come on, you.

BOYD. I can't move.

MICK. You let my father run, it's your turn now. You get the same chance.

BOYD. Where's your idealism now?

MICK. It died with my baby.

BOYD. So then you start blowing up babies. Some fucking progress. I'm not going anywhere with you.

WILLIE. Your Ma and Da are upstairs. He'll torch the place with you and them in it. It's up to you.

BOYD. Aye.

WILLIE. You should have had a son Boyd, it might have been different.

BOYD. I'm glad I didn't. He'd only have got his throat cut. C'mon. Let's get it over with.

They go out. A terrific whoosh of flame outside. Daylight. VICTOR *and* KATE *creep down. It is quiet.* HIS REV. *comes in.*

HIS REV. I have to tell you your son is dead.

KATE. Oh no.

HIS REV. Burned to death trying to protect you. He made the ultimate loyal sacrifice for you. Victor, it is a sign from God. It must be God's inheritance.

KATE. Victor, don't believe him.

HIS REV. Come to the church, Victor, there is comfort there.

KATE. Don't leave me here alone, Victor.

VICTOR *goes out with* HIS REV. *A broken figure.* ANNE *comes on with a suitcase. Overcoat on.*

Where are you going?

ANNE. Anywhere. Anywhere that isn't here.

KATE. What about Mick?

ANNE. He's not the boy I knew.

KATE. They broke my clock. Why did they break my clock?

She starts to weep. ANNE *comforts her and takes her off.* SOLDIERS *come on and slump down.*

OFFICER. Well that was a right fuck up. I despair of these people.

SERGEANT. What do we do now, sir?

OFFICER. We now have to rule the place ourselves. They're not fit to govern themselves. And we have to catch the rats that are gnawing at those foundations.

MICK *comes in.*

SERGEANT. Here's one of them now.

MICK. I have come to complain about the atrocities committed by your men.

OFFICER. Have you now? Sergeant.

SERGEANT *grabs* MICK .

Put him back in the cage and leave him there.

MICK. On what charge?

OFFICER. We'll find one. I am sure someone could be persuaded to inform on you.

MICK. Why don't you ever listen to us?

OFFICER. I did. Where did it get me? Take him.

They rush MICK *out. He sees clock.*

Tut tut, a perfectly good clock.

SOLDIERS *back. One turns on the radio. Blasting pop. They encamp in the place, making it a tip.* KATE *comes on, has to pick her way through them. Carries a meal on a tray out to* MICK. *Comes back with the full tray.*

KATE (*to* OFFICER). He refuses to eat.

He can't hear and she has to keep shouting over the music. He hears it at last. Goes out. OFFICER *comes back with a shrug. Sits and drinks. She goes off. Carries another full tray out, comes back with it. Looks at him. He shrugs. Music ends. Light change.* WILLIE *comes on. Sits with* OFFICER.

OFFICER. What is that cleric up to?

WILLIE. He's got Victor building him another church. As a memorial to Boyd. Victor has gone loop the loop. He's wired up to the galaxy. If your man out here does starve himself to death there'll be hell to pay.

OFFICER. He won't. He won't have the stomach for it.

WILLIE. He might.

OFFICER. Let the police handle it. There's none of my men in the front line anymore so you can go ahead and kill each other.

WILLIE. What the hell do you want here? All you ever do is sit around talking about the security problem? You can't defeat this kind of terror. You have to deal with it.

OFFICER. It is a security problem. We have to protect our interests. Keep me informed.

Hands over money and WILLIE *goes out.* KATE *comes on.*

KATE. He refuses to eat. He refuses to wear your prison clothes. He says he is a political prisoner not a criminal in a cage.

OFFICER. That's up to him.

KATE. You can't let him die.

OFFICER. That's up to him.

KATE. You can't.

OFFICER. What difference will it make?

KATE. Don't you have any mercy? Don't you want the state and the law to be seen to be fair for everyone?

OFFICER. No law is being broken. An individual, properly sentenced in a court, has made an individual choice. As an act of intimidation and blackmail and as a challenge to authority.

KATE. What is the state then? Authority or a just law?

OFFICER. Laws enacted by authority. Let him starve. He'll soon come to his senses and see it is not worth fighting for.

KATE. So you will just stand by?

OFFICER. Yes.

KATE. I want you people out of this house, my house. I can't live like this. Look at it. My home. The state of it.

OFFICER. Then learn to keep it in order. We don't want to be here.

KATE. Then why are you here?

OFFICER. Following orders. Protecting you.

KATE. This is not my home anymore.

OFFICER. Speak to your husband about it, not me. He asked us in here. It is up to him.

KATE. Aye. I'm just a woman. You pay no heed to me.

OFFICER. Kate, if you want him to live then wait until he is past the point of rationality and then as his family you can take on the decision for him to continue to let him die or for us to feed him. I will have the paper ready here for you to sign. You decide. Goodnight.

He goes out and SOLDIERS *follow. Darkening.* VICTOR *comes in.*

KATE. Victor. Have you seen the state of him out there?

VICTOR. Aye.

KATE. We cannot let this happen. He's our own family.

VICTOR. Yours, not mine.

KATE. We are long past that. We are all responsible. You must get them to stop it.

VICTOR. How can I stop it? I couldn't stop my own son from being killed? Because I listened to you. By giving in to you was I the ink on his death warrant? What do you say to that? Did we kill our son by our deeds? And you ask me still to be responsible. To save your family when I couldn't save my own. It is up to him. Let him take his turn at suffering.

KATE. It will lead to murder.

OFFICER. Everything leads to murder here.

KATE. I want those damned soldiers out of my house.

VICTOR. If they go we will have no house.

KATE. We can't live like this.

VICTOR. Then don't ask me, ask him out there to give up his bloody protest and his futile war.

KATE. He can only do that if you give him what he wants.

VICTOR. That's just blackmail. He wants what was never his.

KATE. Mine, mine too. Who are you going to leave it to, Victor?

VICTOR. You'll find out.

KATE. I have a right to know.

VICTOR. Right? Right? It's all I bloody hear. The right to murder my son? The right to steal his inheritance? What kind of bloody right is that?

KATE. I never again want to hear you say, my son. He was mine as much as ever he was yours. I have a right as great as yours. Once and for all. What are you going to do with this place?

HIS REV. *walks in.*

HIS REV. He is going to leave it to his church. Is that not so, Victor. So that our church and this land will be safe for the worship and glory of God and his chosen people.

KATE. Victor, you can't.

HIS REV. Who else would inherit it? Your daughter and that rat out in his cage? That is unthinkable. We all know what you would do if you had it. That church would be torn down and the congregation left to flee before the fires of your hate.

KATE. No, I don't think that would happen but there is no point in my saying that to you because you have the world stitched to your own pattern and nobody can unpick it. You cannot sacrifice all of us on his altar, Victor, you cannot.

VICTOR. Leave me be. It is God's wish.

KATE. That's an excuse. You have to look in your own heart. Make your own choice.

HIS REV. *puts documents and a pen on the table.*

HIS REV. I have the papers here. sign them, Victor. Create the rock and the foundation of our faith . . .

VICTOR. Will you shut up? I'm talking to my wife. Jesus but you love the sound of your own voice and all the big words. Will you give it a rest for a minute? You fart like the rest of us. Kate, what do I do? I'm asking you, I'm not telling you. Where's Anne?

KATE. She has gone.

VICTOR. Have we lost them all?

KATE. There is still that boy out there.

VICTOR. He has lost himself. We tried, Kate. Look what it brought us.

KATE. We did what they told us. We were wrong. We should learn from that. It has to come from our hearts. We have to find a way for all of us to be together, Victor, if our life is to be worth anything.

VICTOR. How?

KATE. You can start by having mercy on that boy.

VICTOR. Will he have mercy on me?

HIS REV. You cannot give in to that blackmail. We won't allow it.

KATE. Will you get out of this house and leave us alone?

HIS REV. I was born here, I live here too. Now tell me this, in all your wisdom, can you reconcile me and that man out there so that we can both live here? No, you can't. You never will. So you have to choose between us.

KATE. But you profess a God of mercy.

HIS REV. I profess a faith and I defend it. Victor . . .

KATE. Get out of here and leave my man alone.

VICTOR. Kate, it doesn't matter. It doesn't matter what we might want, they'll decide it for us.

HIS REV. Not if you sign these papers.

KATE *takes them and tears them up.*

KATE. Now will you go?

VICTOR. You heard the wife.

HIS REV. *walks out.*

I think I'll go in and lie down. I'm tired, Kate.

KATE. I'll get you a cup of tea. You go on in.

He goes off. Light change. OFFICER *comes on and puts a paper on the table.*

KATE. How is he?

OFFICER. He doesn't have very much longer.

KATE. Is there no reprieve?

OFFICER. Not from us. We have strong government again, Kate. No his only reprieve would be from you.

VICTOR *comes on.*

Will you sign the paper when the time comes?

VICTOR. What paper?

OFFICER. He out there will soon be past the coherent responsibility for himself. He will linger a while like that. He can be revived. That is up to Kate. As his closest kin it falls to her not us to decide if he lives or dies.

VICTOR. Do it. You ask me for mercy. If you let him die for his cause you make it your cause. That would be the end of reconcilement.

OFFICER. What do you want, Kate? Will you come and see the man outside?

KATE. I will.

OFFICER. You can talk to him.

KATE. Aye. That's kind of you. To allow me. It seems all we can do is what you allow us.

OFFICER. We are only trying to help.

KATE. Aye. Well I will allow Mick the dignity of his own choice. You can put your papers away.

She and OFFICER *go out. A wailing from off-stage. There is a string of distant explosions.* WILLIE *comes on full of energy, looks around the empty house.*

WILLIE. Aye we could fix that up. Get rid of that oul clock.

He takes a gun out, checks, with a satisfying snap. Lays it on table. Takes another one out. The same with it. HIS REV. *comes on.*

What do you want here?

HIS REV. I could ask you the same? What do you want?

WILLIE. I'll tell you what I don't want. I don't want to be trotting at your coat tails so that you can threaten and bluster about what all we might do if you don't get your way. I've done enough of your dirty work. And I don't want to end up wasting in a cage like Mick.

HIS REV. Then what do you want?

WILLIE. Legitimacy. I've always been the bastard boy here. With no right or claim. Well, I want legitimacy and Victor is going to give it to me.

HIS REV. How?

WILLIE. It's simple. He has no son to defend him or build this place up again. He can adopt me as his son and heir. I'll look after it. I'll be legitimate. Victor, come out here. I want to talk to you.

VICTOR *comes out with* KATE .

VICTOR (*looks at* HIS REV.). I want no more advice.

WILLIE. No, you want help, and I'm here to give it to you. Victor, you have nobody left belonging to you. No son, grandson, nothing. Well. I'm here. Take me as your son. I'll look after you. I'll look after you both. I'm the only one strong enough to do it. I'll build it up again, missus, and you can sit by the fire. What do you say? I'm all that's left. What do you say?

VICTOR *walks forward and looks at the guns.*

VICTOR. What do I say? I'd rather shoot myself.

WILLIE. Think about it? You'll see it makes sense. You won't want to give up this place.

VICTOR. Is this what we are come to, Mother?

WILLIE. I'll buy a new clock. Money no object.

VICTOR. I don't want a new clock.

WILLIE *goes and picks up his guns.*

WILLIE. Maybe I'll buy you one anyway. I asked you. I made you an offer. Now I'm telling you. I'm taking over the business. (*Smiles.*) I'm the new Godfather.

There is a loud banging on the door. WILLIE *pockets the guns and steps behind door.* KATE *goes and opens door. The* SERGEANT *is there.*

SERGEANT. Excuse me, there's someone here come to see you. She wants to know if she can come in.

KATE *looks past him.*

KATE. Of course she can come in. Anne, darling, come here to me.

ANNE steps in. KATE embraces her and we see she is heavily pregnant.

He's dead.

ANNE. I know. I didn't want to come back. But I had to.

KATE. Is the child you're carrying his?

ANNE. It is. A grandson for you, Victor. It must be a boy, he kicks like one. With both feet. Can I stay, Daddy?

VICTOR. I never wanted you to go. Go inside.

ANNE and KATE go in. VICTOR stares at the other two. They all remember the night of the smothering.

I will ask you two to go.

He follows them in.

WILLIE. What the hell, we did it once we can do it again. Are you with me?

HIS REV. I have no part in this.

WILLIE. You were there the last time. Or have your forgotten that?

HIS REV. He won't let you.

WILLIE. He's an old man. I'll see you around, Reverend.

He goes out. VICTOR comes back.

VICTOR. Are you still here?

HIS REV. Now, surely you must give it to me.

VICTOR. You'll have to take it. And you'll have to deal with him that was your lackey first. Think about that.

HIS REV. goes out. VICTOR gets the clock and puts it on the table. Sits with it.

I wonder now is there some say of fixing this.

Starts to tinker with it. Quiet. Then the birth cries of a new baby off. He lifts his head and listens. Puts the clock, unfixed, back up. Goes out. He comes back tenderly holding the baby in a basket. Sets it down. KATE follows. Peers at baby.

KATE. You see who he looks like?

VICTOR. I have a name for him. We'll call him John.

KATE. We'll call him what she wants to call him.

VICTOR. We'll call him John and that's an end of it. I'm telling you.

KATE. Yes, Victor.

VICTOR. Is she all right?

KATE. She is.

VICTOR. So will this boy be too. I'll make sure of it. I'll mind him. You go to bed.

KATE. Are you feared for him, Victor?

VICTOR. Never you mind. You go to bed.

HIS REV. and WILLIE *appear outside in the shadows. As she turns to go in her attention is attracted.*

KATE. Is there somebody out there?

Goes to look. They step back hidden.

Just a trick of the light. Are you all right, Victor?

VICTOR. Aye. I'll just sit for a while.

KATE. Good night.

She goes off. HIS REV. *and* WILLIE *move forward. Then pull back as* VICTOR *goes and looks out. He brings out his rifle and goes again to look at the baby. Outside.*

WILLIE. You are coming in there with me.

HIS REV. I will not.

WILLIE. I am not having you staying out here knowing what will happen. You will betray me as soon as the deed is done. I want you part of it. Or are you here to stop me?

HIS REV. What is one life against the preservation of the church of God?

WILLIE. As long as it's somebody else's life. Just another sacrifice to the greater glory, eh? I ought to shoot you. Do you not fancy dying for your faith?

HIS REV. Must it be done? Is there no other way?

WILLIE. Oh, I'll :narry Anne. It will be arranged. I just don't want to bring up somebody else's child.

VICTOR is creeping to the door. Gun ready. WILLIE *takes out his gun.*

WILLIE. Come on.

HIS REV. I've got to . . . I've got to relieve myself . . .

WILLIE. Shitting yourself are you? That's no surprise.

> VICTOR *flings the door open.* WILLIE *has his gun and pointed at him just as* VICTOR *has the rifle pointed at him. A frozen moment and then* HIS REV. *legs it away.* WILLIE *laughs.*

WILLIE. Put up the gun, Victor.

VICTOR. You put yours up.

WILLIE. I'm coming into this house whether you like it or not, Victor.

VICTOR. I would die for that boy there.

WILLIE. You may have to. Don't fight it, Victor. I'l see you right. You gave me my start and now I'm what you've got left.

VICTOR. I repented my sins.

WILLIE. Too late now. You've lost your nerve, Victor. You're too old. Put that down.

> *He looks powerful and* VICTOR *looks shaky. Then from off on the border side.*

MARY (*yelling*). Kathleen, Kathleen, will you come out here and help me in. My pains are killing me and it's an awful long step from the car. Kathleen, will you come out and help your own mother.

> WILLIE *puts the gun in his pocket.* VICTOR *lowers his as* KATE *runs out.*

KATE. What in the name of God is happening?

MARY. Kathleen, am I to be left stranded here. Help me.

> KATE *comes leading her on.* MARY *is very old now but rouged up and very well dressed with a big fur collar and hat.* VICTOR *comes round. Lights come up.*

VICTOR. Who the hell invited her?

> OFFICER *appears behind* MARY.

OFFICER. I did. She is your mother-in-law after all. I'm sure she will be welcome here.

MARY. I hope so. I want to see that new wee baby. Where is the darling?

OFFICER. Mary and I have been having some very interesting chats. Since we are both concerned in this family of yours.

MARY. He has been very civil to me. Which is more than can be said for any class of a welcome I had here before. But sure we can put all that behind us.

She is in now.

MARY. Is that the bonny boy? Ah look at him. He's the spit of Gabriel. Now that would be a very good name for it, wouldn't it? Wouldn't you think of calling him Gabriel now.

KATE (*warning look at* VICTOR). That's up to Anne.

MARY. And where is she? I have to see her to congratulate her.

KATE. Come on, Ma.

They go in. Taking the baby.

WILLIE. I will see you later, Victor.

He goes off.

VICTOR. What's going on?

OFFICER (*bellowing*). Sergeant.

SERGEANT *and* SOLDIER *rush on.*

Line up. Attenshun. Now. You've had your orders. Get them off.

They begin to strip off their uniforms.

Come on it's Army property not yours.

VICTOR. Will you tell me what is going on?

OFFICER. The walls have come down. The East has fallen. We have no enemy now. These are the defence cuts. They are out of a job. We have no need of this island now. No need to defend it. Different times, Victor, different interests. Come on, pile them up.

They pile the stuff up. Stand in their pants. OFFICER *throws them two bright tracksuits. They put them on.*

SOLDIER. What's going to happen to us, sir?

OFFICER. Get on your bike and get a job if you can find one. When we're cleared up here. Get on with it.

They lift the pile of uniforms and cart them off. Come back with another table to set up one long table with a cloth. Start clearing their junk out and straightening the room.

VICTOR. But what's happening to us? Here.

OFFICER. We'll sort you out. You'll get compensation of course.

We'll all sit down and sort it out. You can decide what you want
to do. We will be generous. Come on, now, let's have the table
set.

They start laying places and bringing piled plates of food. Heaps of it.
MARY *with* KATE *and* ANNE *come out to sit at the table. Served*
drinks, little things to nibble.

VICTOR. What is she doing here?

OFFICER. To talk. To help. We realised we had to talk to each
other. So long as you felt you could turn to us when your wife
argued with you and as long as she felt she could turn to her
mother to save her when you lifted a fist to her, well, it's no
basis for a stable marriage. You have to be allowed to sort out
your differences. There will be sacrifices of course. Nobody can
get everything they want but that's in the nature of things, isn't
it? But everyone will get something. We are all Europeans now.
We have plans for a one island economy. Investment. Aid.
There may in time be a wider federation. Oh yes. Everybody
satisfied.

VICTOR. But who owns it?

OFFICER. We all do. In trust for the future generations. Come and
sit down and we'll talk about it. There is only ever one end.
Sitting round a table.

HIS REV. *comes in and sits and is served.* VICTOR *glares at him.*

OFFICER. He represents a voice here.

MARY (*leaning over*). Good evening Your Reverence, you are
welcome to our table.

HIS REV. If I don't like anything I hear, I'm not staying. And we
want no unwelcome guests.

MARY. Sure aren't we celebrating a new birth? We have to think of
his future, the future of young Gabriel.

VICTOR. His name is John. Where is that child? I want him with
me.

He takes the bundled baby and cradles him in his arms as he sits.

ANNE. I never agreed to John.

KATE. Let him alone. It's not christened yet. And you, mother, will
you just stop your interfering ways. Fill that with food and a bit
less chat.

HIS REV. There are some who are not here? Are they invited.

ANNE *takes the baby.*

ANNE. He's asleep, da.

Takes baby to a cot down front and goes back to her place.

OFFICER. No they are not invited but they will be dealt with Sergeant. Oh sorry, ex-sergeant. Can you?

SERGEANT goes off and drags on the body of WILLIE by the legs and dumps him down at the front.

We found him. It is very difficult to disentangle who might have killed him. He had so many enemies. Now is everyone getting what they want?

They all settle at the table to feast. Then MICK walks on, looks at it. Steps forward and lifts WILLIE up by the hand.

MICK. Willie.

WILLIE. Ah, Mick. How's about you.

MICK goes and looks in the cradle.

Is he like you?

MICK. Not a whole lot.

WILLIE. No, well, he'll be his own boy.

MICK. Do you know, I've come to a conclusion.

WILLIE. What about?

MICK. I've been thinking about oul Abraham.

WILLIE. Him? I don't know. I've figured and figured and I still don't understand it.

MICK. No, listen. If there is no God . . .

WILLIE. Which there isn't. I mean, if anybody knows there is no God it is us, isn't it.

MICK. God is a dream in men's minds. So the whole idea of God speaking to Abraham was a dream in Abraham's mind. He created the whole situation himself. He told himself what to do. He set out to test himself. He took Isaac up there, he laid him out, and he prepared to kill him, until the voice said, don't do it. And that voice was his own. And he didn't do it. Don't you see?

WILLIE. No.

MICK. He didn't do it. He undreamt his own dream.

WILLIE. So where does that get us?

MICK. If you dream one dream to live by you can undream it

because it is only yours and not unchangeable. That's what
Abraham did. We just didn't understand it.

WILLIE. It's a bit late for us.

MICK. But we're here, Willie. At the feast. And they will have to
undream us. Do you fancy a drink?

WILLIE. Do I?

HIS REV. Who's paying for this?

OFFICER. Don't worry. We are. Enjoy it while you can.

> ANNE *gets up and comes to the cot and kneels by it. Then* VICTOR
> *comes forward to a chair and brings with him the clock and sets to
> fiddling with it.* MICK *and* WILLIE *get a drink and watch while the
> others get on with the feasting.*

ANNE. I have a dream for you little one. That you will understand
your history and the dangerous dreams that made it. And my
dream for you is that you will grow up to be one of the meek.
For they do inherit the earth. They have to. Because they are
the ones who do not seek revenge, they pick up the pieces and
put them back and build again and go on. We tell a wrong
history. We tell of lunatics, or orchestrators of discord. We tell
of wars and battles and crimes and mass murder. We make
heroes and villains. There are heroes. They are not sung about.
They are all the people who did not join and put on a black
shirt or a brown shirt or a blue shirt or claimed a higher power
gave them the right to oppress their neighbour. They are the
people who suffered and endured and comforted each other
and refused to hate, who saw themselves as ordinary and the
same, and picked up the pieces and went on. The meek. Who
deserve better. But their daily small acts of love and kindness
are a tide. I hope you have better. That you will have no dreams
to torment you. That you will see that we all of us have a choice.
We can say good morning instead of passing by. We can not lift
a gun, we can take back the bitter words, we can perform those
small acts of love that are our own salvation.

VICTOR. I think I've fixed this. It's going. Can you hear it.

> *They all listen.*

KATE. I hear nothing. You could never fix anything.

VICTOR. I'm telling you it's going.

KATE. Will you leave that for somebody that knows what they're
doing. What do you know about clocks?

VICTOR. Will you stop going on at me and listen to the bloody
thing. Can you not hear it?

KATE. He won't give in to me. He'd rather sit there and pretend that thing was ticking when none of us can hear it. Will you come back here and sit down.

VICTOR. I can hear it. I can hear it ticking. Time goes on.